· TROPHIES ·

Practice Book

Grade 5

Harcourt

Orlando   Boston   Dallas   Chicago   San Diego

Visit *The Learning Site!*
www.harcourtschool.com

ISBN 13: 978-0-15-323526-9   ISBN 10: 0-15-323526-8

26 27 28 29 30   0982   12 11 10 09

Contents

DISTANT VOYAGES

▶ From the list above the chart, find two synonyms for each
Vocabulary Word. Write them in columns two and three.
In the fourth column, write your own synonym for the word.

| master | fatigued | oath | expert | turmoil |
| memento | disturbance | wearied | remembrance | pledge |

Vocabulary Word	Synonym	Synonym	My Synonym
souvenir			
exhausted			
commotion			
vow			
authority			

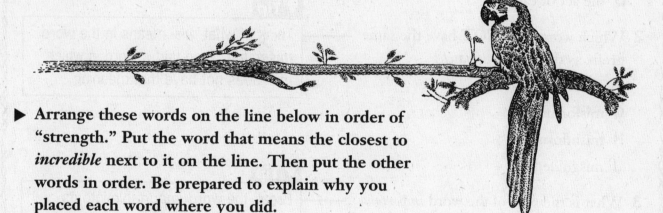

▶ Arrange these words on the line below in order of
"strength." Put the word that means the closest to
incredible next to it on the line. Then put the other
words in order. Be prepared to explain why you
placed each word where you did.

surprising   uncommon   ordinary   unusual   amazing

incredible					

TRY THIS! Think of a new pet you and your family members would like to have. Work together to write three sentences to describe that pet. Use at least three Vocabulary Words in your sentences.

Name _____

▶ **Read the paragraph. Circle the letter of the best answer to each question.**

When deciding on a pet, be careful to make a realistic choice. A Great Dane would be a mismatch for someone with a tiny apartment. If you are always late, don't choose a pet that must be walked on time. If you are thinking about adopting an exotic animal, realize that many rare birds and mammals are not importable into the United States. Ask a good pet-store owner for more information.

1 What is the meaning of the word *careful*?

  A full of care

  B not caring

  C a full car

  D the act of caring

> 💡 **Tip**
> Combine the meaning of the root word with that of the suffix.

2 Which word does NOT have the same prefix as the word *mismatch*?

  F miser

  G misfortune

  H misinform

  J misguided

> 💡 **Tip**
> Think of what *mis-* means in the word *mismatch*. Then find a word in which *mis-* does not have that meaning.

3 What is the root of the word *importable* in the final sentence?

  A im

  B port

  C portable

  D able

> 💡 **Tip**
> Break the word *importable* into its smallest units of meaning. After you have identified the prefix and the suffix, the root is what you have left.

SCHOOL-HOME CONNECTION Help your child form new words by adding one prefix and one or more suffixes to these words: *happy, help, depend, honest.* See how many new words he or she can form from each word.

2

Practice Book
Distant Voyages

© Harcourt

Name _____

▶ **Read each passage. Then answer the questions. Choose from the following points of view:** *first person, third-person limited,* **and** *third-person omniscient.*

Bolivia needs to find a way to become friends with Rory and Derek. She decides to use Lucette to help her out. Bolivia figures that if she can get the boys to help her catch Lucette, her problem will be solved.

1. What is the point of view of the paragraph? _____

2. What helped you to identify the point of view? _____

_____

"I'm not sure whether I want to be friends with Bolivia. Derek and I had such great plans for the summer, but now my mother is planning this cookout where we can both meet Bolivia. It'll be hard, but I bet we can avoid her if we try."

3. What is the point of view of the paragraph? _____

4. What helped you to identify the point of view? _____

_____

Rory did not want to get to know Bolivia. He thought for a while. Then he realized Bolivia did not have a pool pass. He thought, "The pool is a great place to escape her for a while."

Bolivia, however, had other plans. She decided to let Lucette out. She thought, "Rescuing Lucette will be a sure way to get the boys' interest."

5. What is the point of view of the paragraphs?

_____

6. What helped you identify point of view?

_____

_____

Practice Book
Distant Voyages

© Harcourt

The Hot and
Cold Summer

Grammar:
Declarative and
Interrrogative
Sentences

Skill Reminder **A sentence** expresses a complete thought.
Declarative sentences make statements and end with
periods. **Interrogative sentences** ask questions and end
with question marks.

▶ Read each group of words. If it is a sentence, write whether it is *declarative* or
interrogative. If it is not a complete sentence, add words to make a declarative or
interrogative sentence. Tell which kind of sentence you created.

1. Both boys piled their plates with food. _____

2. Couldn't understand his mother. _____

_____

3. Did Bolivia have red hair? _____

4. What kind of frosting? _____

5. The burgers had bean sprouts in them. _____

▶ Rewrite each sentence correctly, using capital letters and end marks. Then write
declarative or *interrogative* to tell what kind of sentence it is.

6. last summer Bolivia and her family traveled _____

_____

7. who caught Lucette _____

8. what was so special about Lucette _____

_____

TRY THIS! Work with a family member to write three declarative sentences. Then rewrite them
as interrogative sentences.

Name _____

Skill Reminder • Short *a* can be spelled *a*. • Short *i* can be spelled *i, u,* or *ui*. • Short *e* can be spelled *ea*. • Short *u* can be spelled *o, oe,* or *o-e*.

▶ Fold the paper along the dotted line. As each spelling word is read aloud, write it in the blank. Then unfold your paper, and check your work. Practice spelling any words you missed.

1. _____
2. _____
3. _____
4. _____
5. _____
6. _____
7. _____
8. _____
9. _____
10. _____
11. _____
12. _____
13. _____
14. _____
15. _____
16. _____
17. _____
18. _____
19. _____
20. _____

SPELLING WORDS

1. master
2. ahead
3. build
4. front
5. meant
6. bread
7. ready
8. busy
9. quit
10. mother
11. above
12. does
13. advantage
14. business
15. sweater
16. plastic
17. balance
18. limit
19. among
20. dozen

© Harcourt

5

▶ **Read the Vocabulary Words. Then write the Vocabulary Word that best completes each sentence.**

| tread | exaggerate | moss | sternly | quiver | compose |

The hike in the woods offered something for everyone. Nick, who sometimes made up stories, did not **(1)** _____ this time when he said the trail was steep and rugged. Kaitlyn, who liked to watch animals, had a **(2)** _____ so quiet that she was able to sneak up close to a deer. Kim noticed **(3)** _____ growing on the tree trunks and rocks.

When the group reached the clearing, Nick spoke commands **(4)** _____ to keep everyone in order. Then he set up a target and pulled an arrow from the **(5)** _____ on his back. Before he drew the bowstring, he took a deep breath to **(6)** _____ himself.

▶ **Write the Vocabulary Word that best completes each analogy.**

7. *Happily* is to *gladly* as *strictly* is to _____.

8. *Stir up* is to *excite* as *calm down* is to _____.

9. *Soil* is to *flower* as *tree trunk* is to _____.

10. *Hand* is to *touch* as *foot* is to _____.

11. *Paper* is to *briefcase* as *arrow* is to _____.

12. *Whisper* is to *shout* as *understate* is to _____.

TRY THIS! Choose a Vocabulary Word. If the word is a noun, write three adjectives that go with it. If it is a verb, write three adverbs. If it is an adverb, write three verbs.

© Harcourt

Name _____

▶ **Read the paragraph. Then circle the letter of the best answer to each question.**

George loved to compete in sports. He had always been the highest scorer on Peyton High's basketball team. There had never been a better guard in the history of the school. But George's basketball career was about to change. This week he and his family were moving from their small town of Carthage, Illinois, to the big city of Boston, Massachusetts. His new school would have thousands of students. George wondered whether he would even get to play on the team.

1 If this paragraph is the beginning of a story, what will the story be about?

   A whether George will like his new school

   B what will happen to George's family in Boston

   C a comparison of small towns and big cities

   D George trying to make the team

> **Tip**
> Think about the main idea of this paragraph. In what direction will the story probably go from here?

2 What problem, or conflict, will George likely encounter in the story?

   F having people make fun of him because he is from a small town

   G getting lost in his new school

   H proving that he is good enough to be on the team

   J understanding people's accents

> **Tip**
> If necessary, reread the last few lines of the paragraph to see what problem George is worried about.

3 What evidence suggests that George will overcome his problem?

   A Stories always have happy endings.

   B People from small towns always succeed in cities.

   C George is a stubborn person.

   D George loves to compete and is an excellent player.

> **Tip**
> Notice the things that the author tells about George.

SCHOOL-HOME CONNECTION Discuss with your child another story he or she has read, such as "The Hot and Cold Summer." Have your child talk about the main conflict in that story and how it is resolved.

7

Practice Book
Distant Voyages

© Harcourt

Name _____

▶ **Read each passage. Then read the question, and circle the letter of the best answer.**

Our solar system consists of the sun and all the bodies that orbit around it. Nine planets orbit the sun, and many of these planets have satellites that circle them. Also orbiting the sun are more asteroids and comets than we can count.

1 Which genre description best fits this passage?

A narrative nonfiction

B realistic fiction

C expository nonfiction

Finally, Dr. Summerford and the rest of the crew were ready to head into the bush. All the difficulties they had experienced would fade if they could locate a pride of lions. The jeeps headed off, and the heavily laden scientists followed.

2 Which genre description best fits this passage?

F narrative nonfiction

G fantasy

H expository nonfiction

Squeeblets were small, sticky balls of a substance that looked like licorice. They didn't talk, they didn't move, yet somehow Potophor knew they were intelligent. He turned on his proto-translator hoping that the sensitive instrument could pick up their thoughts.

3 Which genre description best fits this passage?

A expository nonfiction

B drama

C fiction

▶ **Explain the difference between expository nonfiction and narrative nonfiction.**

_____

_____

_____

SCHOOL-HOME CONNECTION With your child, search through a magazine and find a nonfiction article. Read the article together. Then help your child to write a fictional version of the article.

8

Practice Book
Distant Voyages

© Harcourt

Name _____

Skill Reminder • An **imperative sentence** gives a command or makes a request. The subject is *you* (understood). The sentence ends with a period. • An **exclamatory sentence** expresses strong feeling. It ends with an exclamation point.

▶ Write whether each sentence is *imperative* or *exclamatory*.

1. Imagine the color of the moss. _____

2. How blurry it looks! _____

3. Try to concentrate. _____

4. How delicious corn cakes are! _____

▶ Rewrite the following sentences, adding capital letters and end marks. Then in parentheses ( ), write the type of sentence each one is.

5. try seeing with your ears _____

_____

6. put a cloth over your eyes _____

_____

7. how confusing those noises are _____

_____

8. practice listening carefully _____

_____

TRY THIS! With a partner, look for imperative and exclamatory sentences in comic strips. Copy three imperative and three exclamatory sentences that you find.

Practice Book
Distant Voyages

Name _____

Sees Behind
Trees

Spelling: Words
with Long *a*, *e*,
and *i*

Skill Reminder • The long *a* sound can be spelled *ay* or *ai*.
• The long *e* sound can be spelled *ie* or *ea*. • The long *i* sound
can be spelled *igh* or *y-e*.

▶ Fold the paper along the dotted line. As each spelling word is read aloud, write it
in the blank. Then unfold your paper, and check your work. Practice spelling any
words you missed.

1. _____

2. _____

3. _____

4. _____

5. _____

6. _____

7. _____

8. _____

9. _____

10. _____

11. _____

12. _____

13. _____

14. _____

15. _____

16. _____

17. _____

18. _____

19. _____

20. _____

SPELLING WORDS

1. stayed
2. brain
3. thief
4. meat
5. flight
6. style
7. delighted
8. daily
9. breathe
10. meanwhile
11. believes
12. tonight
13. increased
14. explained
15. slightly
16. payment
17. brief
18. tray
19. byte
20. raise

© Harcourt

Practice Book
Distant Voyages

Name _____

▶ **As you read the paragraph, use context clues to determine the meaning of each Vocabulary Word in dark print. Then write the Vocabulary Word that matches each definition.**

Keiko had been practicing for the ballet **audition** for weeks. When her turn to perform came, the piano **accompanist**, Mimi, played **simultaneously** as Keiko danced. The musical **accompaniment** Mimi played was a favorite piece, a piano **sonata.** Halfway through the piece, Mimi **grimaced** as she struck a wrong note. She kept playing, and Keiko continued to dance without missing a beat.

1. a tryout for a performing role _____

2. musical piece for one or two instruments _____

3. music that is played along with another's performance

_____

4. twisted the face as if in pain _____

5. person who plays music while another person performs

_____

6. happening at the same time _____

▶ **Write the Vocabulary Word that fits with each group of words.**

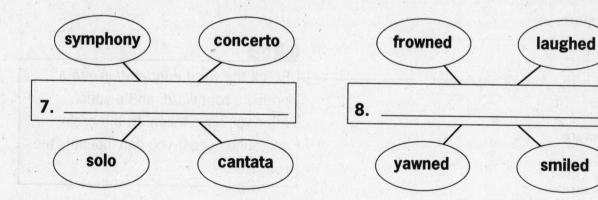

symphony   concerto   frowned   laughed

7. _____   **8.** _____

solo   cantata   yawned   smiled

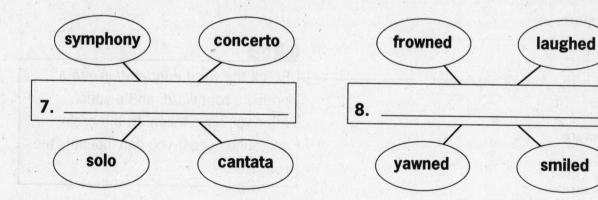

Write a paragraph about either a musical performance you attended or a favorite CD. Use at least three Vocabulary Words.

11

© Harcourt

Name _____

▶ **Read the paragraph. Then circle the letter of the best answer to each question.**

The human voice was the first musical instrument. People could sing long before they created harps or violins. The voice has remained an incredible multipurpose instrument. It can submerge a listener in sound and transport him or her to unimagined places. A musical chorus is made from voices joined in cooperation with each other, but many musical performers are soloists. What would contemporary music be like without singers? It's nonsense to even think about.

1 What is the meaning of *multipurpose*?

   A few purposes

   B no purposes

   C one purpose

   D many purposes

> 💡 **Tip**
> Combine the meaning of the root word with the meaning of the prefix.

2 Which answer choice has a similar meaning to *submerge*?

   F subtract

   G put under

   H support

   J make sick

> 💡 **Tip**
> Do not be fooled by a word part. You are looking for a word meaning.

3 What is the root of *cooperation*?

   A co

   B operate

   C coop

   D operation

> 💡 **Tip**
> Break the word *cooperation* into a prefix, a root word, and a suffix. After you have taken off the prefix and suffix, see if you can indentify the root word.

Practice Book
Distant Voyages

© Harcourt

Name _____

Skill Reminder • Every sentence has a subject and a predicate. The **subject** tells who or what the sentence is about. The **predicate** tells what the subject is or does.
• The **complete subject** includes all the words in the subject.
• The **simple subject** is the main word in the complete subject.

▶ Draw a line between the complete subject and the predicate in the following sentences.

1. Mary wants to play in a chamber orchestra some day.

2. Mary's father supports their local chamber orchestra.

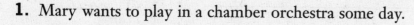

▶ Underline the complete subject in each sentence. Then write the simple subject in the blank.

3. Mary prefers the cello over all other instruments. _____

4. A cello is a stringed instrument. _____

5. The pitch of a cello is lower than that of a viola. _____

6. Both instruments require lots of practice to sound good. _____

▶ Add a complete subject to these sentences. Then circle the simple subject in each sentence.

7. _____ rehearsed on Monday.

8. _____ became ill.

9. _____ were quiet while Holly played.

10. _____ won the first place medal.

 TRY THIS! Copy four declarative sentences from "Yang the Third and Her Impossible Family." Underline the complete subject of each once. Underline the simple subject twice.

13

© Harcourt

Skill Reminder • The long *o* sound can be spelled *o, ou,* or *-e.*
• The long *u* sound can be spelled *o-e, ue, u-e, ui,* or *ui-e.*

▶ Fold the paper along the dotted line. As each spelling word is read aloud, write it in the blank. Then unfold your paper, and check your work. Practice spelling any words you missed.

1. _____

2. _____

3. _____

4. _____

5. _____

6. _____

7. _____

8. _____

9. _____

10. _____

11. _____

12. _____

13. _____

14. _____

15. _____

16. _____

17. _____

18. _____

19. _____

20. _____

SPELLING WORDS
1. soul
2. smoke
3. move
4. clue
5. fruits
6. lose
7. chose
8. stole
9. prove
10. produce
11. juice
12. drove
13. Tuesday
14. rescue
15. continue
16. issue
17. ego
18. argue
19. cruise
20. toll

Practice Book
Distant Voyages

© Harcourt

Name _____

▶ Read the Vocabulary Words. Then read each set of words listed below. Write the Vocabulary Word that is similar to the words in each set.

correspondence	ridiculed	potential	dignity
inspire	counsel	mentor	

1. message; stationery; pen pal; e-mail _____

2. taunted; jeered; mocked; derided _____

3. spur; motivate; hearten; encourage _____

4. advise; direct; guide; instruct _____

5. teacher; coach; trainer; tutor _____

6. possibility; likelihood; capability; ability _____

7. nobility; honor; self-respect; distinction _____

▶ Write the Vocabulary Word that best completes each sentence.

8. Mrs. Parks has _____ with children from many places in the world.

9. She has been a _____ to people most of her life.

10. Mrs. Parks encourages students to work to their

_____.

11. She tells them not to be afraid to be

_____.

12. No matter how she is treated, Mrs. Parks

acts with _____.

Practice Book
Distant Voyages

Name _____

▶ **Read the paragraph. Then circle the letter of the best answer to each question.**

Rosa Parks had some advice for a young man who told her he was having trouble asking questions. She told him that even though she was 83, she was still learning and asking questions. For instance, she said that she was fascinated by new technology, such as computers. Then she told him that she was taking water aerobics and swimming lessons. Her advice to the young man was to gather his nerve and start to ask questions. In her opinion, this was the only way he would learn.

1 What judgment about Rosa Parks is supported by evidence in the paragraph?

  A She still wants to learn new things.

  B She doesn't like asking questions.

  C She is a computer expert.

  D She does not like swimming.

 Tip
Choose the statement that most accurately reflects the information you find in the paragraph.

2 Which of the following pieces of evidence best supports this judgment?

  F Rosa Parks states an opinion.

  G Rosa Parks gives advice.

  H Rosa Parks talks to a young man.

  J Rosa Parks is fascinated by new technology.

Tip
What information about what Rosa Parks likes or does best describes the kind of person she is?

3 What other judgment can you make about Rosa Parks based on the evidence in the paragraph?

  A She does not know how to ask questions.

  B She has lots of nerve.

  C She is a great letter writer.

  D She does not approve of young men who are afraid.

Tip
Look for a statement that can be verified by information in the paragraph.

SCHOOL-HOME CONNECTION Ask your child to write a paragraph about a judgement he or she made about something. Have your child share the paragraph with a family member.

16

Practice Book
Distant Voyages

© Harcourt

Skill Reminder • The **complete predicate** includes all the words that tell what the subject of the sentence is or does.
• The **simple predicate** is the main word or words in the complete predicate.

▶ Underline the complete predicate in each of the following sentences. Write the simple predicate on the line.

1. Adrienne's teacher told the class about Rosa Parks. _____

2. Mrs. Parks is 83 years old. _____

3. Adrienne's great-grandmother celebrated her 85th birthday. _____

▶ Write *complete predicate* or *simple predicate* in the blanks below to identify each underlined word or words in the following sentences. If the complete predicate is the same as the simple predicate, write *same*.

4. Jimmy <u>wrote</u> a letter to Mrs. Parks. _____

5. Mrs. Parks <u>shared her opinion with Jimmy</u>. _____

6. "The right questions <u>help</u>." _____

▶ Finish the following sentences by adding complete predicates. Circle the simple predicates.

7. A computer _____.

8. The answer to my letter _____.

Name _____

Skill Reminder • The vowel sound in *car* is usually spelled *ar*.
• The vowel sound in *fort* can be spelled *or* or *ar*. • The vowel sound in *fair* can be spelled *are* or *air*. • The vowel sound in *dirt* can be spelled *ir* or *ear*.
• The second vowel sound in *outward* can be spelled *or* or *ar*.

▶ Fold the paper along the dotted line. As each spelling word is read aloud, write it in the blank. Then unfold your paper, and check your work. Practice spelling any words you missed.

1. _____
2. _____
3. _____
4. _____
5. _____
6. _____
7. _____
8. _____
9. _____
10. _____
11. _____
12. _____
13. _____
14. _____
15. _____
16. _____
17. _____
18. _____
19. _____
20. _____

SPELLING WORDS
1. parts
2. history
3. warning
4. declare
5. despair
6. shirt
7. learning
8. backward
9. border
10. prepared
11. harsh
12. research
13. carnival
14. particular
15. squirrel
16. harmful
17. charms
18. disorder
19. favored
20. remark

© Harcourt

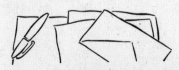

Practice Book
Distant Voyages

Name _____

▶ **Write the Vocabulary Word that best completes each sentence.**

revolution	plunged
ravine	mocking
determination	condolences

1. During a _____, people's lives can change in an instant.

2. The boy _____ into the cold water to cool off from the hot sun.

3. After it fell many feet into a _____, the car was destroyed.

4. The soldier offered _____ to the grieving family.

5. When the movie ended, my brother walked to the car, _____ the silly plot.

6. The soccer team's _____ to win the game grew after they missed their first goal.

▶ **Follow the directions below.**

7. Write a sentence describing your feelings about **revolution**.

_____

8. Write a sentence describing a situation in which you showed **determination**.

_____

TRY THIS! Write a paragraph about a famous *revolution*. You might have to use class resources, such as an encyclopedia, to help you write the paragraph.

Practice Book
Distant Voyages

© Harcourt

Name _____

▶ **Read the paragraph. Then circle the letter of the best answer to each question.**

When Tomás got angry, his black eyes flashed. He was in a bad mood because he had to travel to California on a crowded train with his family. He was hot, and he was tired of being pushed by other passengers. When Mamá asked him to amuse his sister for a while, Tomás sighed. "I don't have to do what you say," he snapped. As Tomás looked in his mother's face, he saw a look of pain cross it. All at once, Tomás realized he should not continue to act that way.

1 What is the setting of this passage?

   A Tomás' home

   B California

   C a bus

   D a train

 Tip
Remember that the setting is the exact place where the story happened.

2 The part of the setting that probably most affected Tomás was

   F the heat and the crowds.

   G being with his family.

   H going to California.

   J the early morning hour.

Tip
Think about the things in the setting that were upsetting Tomás.

3 Which sentence best expresses the theme?

   A People get what they want by being mean.

   B Some people act badly because they don't stop to think.

   C Nobody likes having to care for a younger brother or sister.

   D All people with black, flashing eyes have bad tempers.

Tip
What idea or message do you think the author wants readers to get from this story?

 SCHOOL-HOME CONNECTION Help your child write a paragraph that tells what Tomás does next. Then read the paragraph aloud, and discuss why Tomás behaves the way he does.

Practice Book
Distant Voyages

Skill Reminder   • **A compound subject** is two or more subjects that have the same predicate, usually joined by the conjunction *and* or *or*.   • **A compound predicate** is two or more predicates that have the same subject, usually joined by a conjunction such as *and, but,* or *or.*

▶ **Underline the compound subject in each of the following sentences. Circle the conjunction that joins them.**

1. Chaos and uncertainty were effects of the revolution.

2. Soldiers and their followers journeyed from town to town.

3. The fatigue or poor food weakened the soldiers.

▶ **Underline the compound predicate in each of the following sentences. Circle the conjunction that joins them.**

4. Paco knew the battle was coming but froze with fright.

5. He saw the fighting, got scared, and ran in the opposite direction.

6. Paco's captain was angry and considered punishing him.

▶ **Add a compound subject to sentence 7 and a compound predicate to sentence 8.**

7. _____ disliked war.

8. The soldiers of Pancho Villa _____

_____

TRY THIS! Write five sentences that describe some of your hobbies. Use at least one compound subject and one compound predicate in your sentences.

Skill Reminder • The /s/ sound can be spelled c, s, sc, or ce.
• The /z/ sound can be spelled s or se. • The /sh/ sound can be
spelled ci, ss, ch, or ti.

▶ Fold the paper along the dotted line. As each spelling word is read aloud, write it
in the blank. Then unfold your paper, and check your work. Practice spelling any
words you missed.

1. _____

2. _____

3. _____

4. _____

5. _____

6. _____

7. _____

8. _____

9. _____

10. _____

11. _____

12. _____

13. _____

14. _____

15. _____

16. _____

17. _____

18. _____

19. _____

20. _____

SPELLING WORDS

1. percent
2. absence
3. years
4. refused
5. ancient
6. pressure
7. machine
8. notice
9. scene
10. station
11. social
12. special
13. parachute
14. specialty
15. detention
16. constitution
17. advertisement
18. advise
19. cities
20. chalet

© Harcourt

Practice Book
Distant Voyages

Name _____

▶ As you read the paragraphs, use context clues to determine the meaning of the boldfaced Vocabulary Words. Then use the Vocabulary Words to complete the analogies.

Because he is such a good player, Luis is always in the starting **lineup** when his team plays. As you would expect from the team's **ace** player, his stats are great. If Luis makes an **error**, it comes as a great surprise because he usually plays so well.

The ballpark where Luis plays is **dedicated** to the memory of a famous player. Last year, the ballpark replaced its **artificial** turf with real grass. The park is near an airport, and you can see its **control tower** from the bleachers. The crowd will often watch the planes flying overhead. However, when Luis steps up to the plate no one watches anything but him.

1. *Researcher* is to *laboratory* as *air traffic controller*

is to _____ .

2. *Attempt* is to *try* as *mistake* is to _____ .

3. *Actor* is to *cast* as *starter* is to _____ .

4. *Beginner* is to *learner* as *expert* is to _____ .

5. *Remember* is to *recall* as *devoted* is to _____ .

6. *Play* is to *work* as *real* is to _____ .

▶ Write the Vocabulary Word that best fits each set.

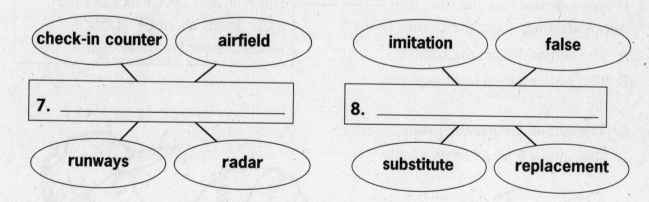

7. _____

check-in counter   airfield   runways   radar

8. _____

imitation   false   substitute   replacement

 TRY THIS! Write a speech you might give to introduce Clemente School's new baseball team. Use at least three Vocabulary Words in your speech.

23

Name _____

▶ **Read the paragraph. Then circle the letter of the best answer to each question.**

Watching the Gomez family in action is like watching a team sport. Just before dinner is ready, Luz and Pepe set the table. Mrs. Gomez makes a salad and serves the side dishes, and Mr. Gomez takes the main course out of the oven. Frances puts Sarita into her highchair. Then the family sit down to eat. After dinner, everyone has a job to do. If working together were an Olympic sport, the Gomez family would win a gold medal.

1 In what way is the Gomez family like a sports team?

> **💡 Tip**
> Think about how the Gomezes act like players on a sports team.

   A Each person has a job to do.

   B The family members compete.

   C Some family members are Olympic athletes.

   D The Gomez family likes sports.

2 Why does the Gomez family deserve a gold medal?

> **💡 Tip**
> Find the sentence in which the author compares the Gomez family to gold medal winners, and see what conclusion you can draw from it.

   F They never fight.

   G Everyone is athletic.

   H They cooperate well.

   J They always have dinner together.

3 Which sentence best describes the author's feelings about the Gomez family?

> **💡 Tip**
> Which answer choice includes the most details about the author's feelings about the Gomezes?

   A The author dislikes the family.

   B The author has no feelings about the family.

   C The author admires the family.

   D The author is afraid of the family.

 **SCHOOL-HOME CONNECTION** Have your child make a list of adjectives that describe the Gomez family, then write a sentence about your family, using an adjective from your list. Have your child share the sentence with a family member.

Practice Book
Distant Voyages

© Harcourt

Name _____

We'll Never
Forget You,
Roberto Clemente

Grammar: Simple
and Compound
Sentences

Skill Reminder • A **simple sentence** expresses only one complete thought. • A **compound sentence** is made up of two or more simple sentences, usually joined by *and, or,* or *but.* Use a comma before the conjunction. • Avoid combining two sentences with nothing, or only a comma, between them.

▶ On the line following each sentence, write *simple sentence* or *compound sentence*.

1. Roberto was sick for much of the season.

_____

2. The big hit would come in September, or Roberto would have to wait till the

next season._____

▶ Combine each pair of simple sentences to form a compound sentence. Be sure to use a comma and an appropriate conjunction (*and, or, but*).

3. Only twenty-six games remained in the season. The fans were hopeful.

_____

_____

4. Game night in Pittsburgh was cold. The rain poured down.

_____

_____

▶ Each sentence is combined incorrectly. Rewrite it correctly.

5. Tom Seaver was pitching for the Mets, Roberto was confident.

_____

_____

6. Seaver would win twenty games Clemente would get his 3,000th hit.

_____

_____

© Harcourt

25

Name _____

Skill Reminder • The /chər/ sound at the end of a word is usually spelled *ture*. • The /zhər/ sound at the end of a word is usually spelled *sure*.

▶ Fold the paper along the dotted line. As each spelling word is read aloud, write it in the blank. Then unfold your paper, and check your work. Practice spelling any words you missed.

1. _____

2. _____

3. _____

4. _____

5. _____

6. _____

7. _____

8. _____

9. _____

10. _____

11. _____

12. _____

13. _____

14. _____

15. _____

16. _____

17. _____

18. _____

19. _____

20. _____

SPELLING WORDS

1. treasure
2. capture
3. feature
4. pleasure
5. measure
6. creature
7. picture
8. adventure
9. mixture
10. structure
11. pasture
12. culture
13. literature
14. furniture
15. temperature
16. legislature
17. immature
18. leisure
19. premature
20. signature

© Harcourt

Practice Book
Distant Voyages

Name _____

▶ **Use the Vocabulary Words to complete the paragraph.**

entrusted	plodded	assured	bountiful	destiny	diligence

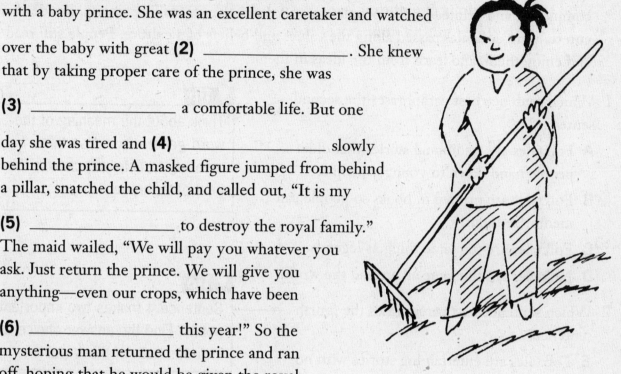

Many centuries ago, a young maid was **(1)** _____ with a baby prince. She was an excellent caretaker and watched over the baby with great **(2)** _____. She knew that by taking proper care of the prince, she was

(3) _____ a comfortable life. But one

day she was tired and **(4)** _____ slowly behind the prince. A masked figure jumped from behind a pillar, snatched the child, and called out, "It is my

(5) _____ to destroy the royal family." The maid wailed, "We will pay you whatever you ask. Just return the prince. We will give you anything—even our crops, which have been

(6) _____ this year!" So the mysterious man returned the prince and ran off, hoping that he would be given the royal family's crops.

▶ **Wrtie the Vocabulary Word that means the opposite of each underlined word.**

7. One year the crop was small and <u>sparse</u>, but the next year it was _____.

8. One year the workers <u>raced</u> through the fields, but the next year they

_____.

TRY THIS! Write three synonyms for the word *plodded*. Then use each synonym in a sentence.

Practice Book
Distant Voyages

Name _____

▶ **Read the paragraph. Then circle the letter of the best answer to each question.**

    People around the world tell folktales. Folktales are legends, myths, and fables that everyone knows and passes down through the generations. Before radio, television, computers, and printed books, people amused themselves by telling stories. Besides being entertaining, folktales passed along the values and beliefs of a culture. People still read and enjoy them, and learn from the ideas in them.

1 Which sentence best paraphrases the second sentence?

  A Folktales are traditional stories that older people hand down to younger people.

  B Folktales are printed in books so people can memorize them.

  C Folktales are the same thing as legends.

  D Folktales are the same all around the world.

> **Tip**
> Think about the meaning of the word *generations*. Use this meaning to help you choose the best paraphrase.

2 Which sentence best paraphrases the fourth sentence?

  F Folktales are entertaining stories with no special meaning.

  G Folktales are more fun to tell than they are to listen to.

  H Folktales are fun to tell and hear, and they express the important ideas of a group.

  J Everyone likes folktales, but many people don't understand why they are important.

> **Tip**
> Sentence 4 makes two important points. Find the answer choice that includes both of these points.

3 Which is the best summary of the paragraph?

  A People rarely tell folktales to other people anymore.

  B People like to watch stories on television.

  C People in many parts of the world tell folktales.

  D Folktales are entertaining stories from the past that still teach important ideas.

> **Tip**
> Choose the answer that best describes the ideas in the paragraph.

© Harcourt

 SCHOOL-HOME CONNECTION Discuss with your child the kind of information that goes into a summary. Then help him or her summarize a favorite story or fairytale.

Practice Book
Distant Voyages

Name _____

▶ **Choose the best meaning for each example of figurative language. Write the answer on the line.**

1. In the moonlight, the road was a white ribbon stretching across the land.

  A The road was narrow and long and shone in the moonlight.

  B The road was dark in spite of the moonlight.

_____

2. The sun set like a golden coin dropping into a slot.

  A A good sunset is worth its weight in gold.

  B When the sun set, it disappeared quickly.

_____

3. The woman was a shadow of her former self.

  A The woman looked thinner than she had been.

  B The woman liked to stand in the dark.

_____

▶ **Read each definition and example of figurative language. Then write your own example.**

4. A **simile** is a comparison between two different things. It uses the words *like* or *as* to compare them: The orange juice looked like liquid sunshine.

_____

_____

5. A **metaphor** is a comparison between two different things. It doesn't use the words *like* or *as* to compare them: Clare's hair is an inky black rope.

_____

_____

SCHOOL-HOME CONNECTION Have your child write a paragraph describing an item in your home. Ask him or her to use two examples of figurative language in the paragraph.

29

Practice Book
Distant Voyages

© Harcourt

Skill Reminder • **A clause** is a group of words with a subject and a predicate; it is used as part of a sentence. • **An independent clause** can stand alone as a sentence. • **A dependent clause** cannot stand alone as a sentence. Dependent clauses often begin with connecting words such as *before, after, because, when,* or *although.*

▶ The sentences below have one or two clauses. Underline each independent clause once. Underline each dependent clause twice.

1. When Princess Asana woke that morning, her heart was filled with hope.

2. Perhaps today she and Shavan could travel to a faraway land.

3. After she yawned and stretched, the princess began

   washing her face in water from a flowered bowl.

4. Suddenly an unusual figure rose from the bowl of water.

▶ Rewrite each item, adding either a dependent clause to an independent clause or an independent clause to a dependent clause.

5. As Asana began to cry _____

   _____

6. "You will be freed from this prison" _____

   _____

7. After she heard these words _____

   _____

8. She then began to smile _____

   _____

Reread a story you have read before. List the independent and dependent clauses.

Practice Book
Distant Voyages

© Harcourt

Skill Reminder • For root words ending with e, drop the e before adding *-ed* or *-ing*. • For root words ending with *ie*, change the *ie* to y before adding *-ing*. • For root words ending with y preceded by a consonant, change the y to *i* before adding *-ed*. • For most other root words, simply add the ending.

▶ Fold the paper along the dotted line. As each spelling word is read aloud, write it in the blank. Then unfold your paper, and check your work. Practice spelling any words you missed.

1. _____
2. _____
3. _____
4. _____
5. _____
6. _____
7. _____
8. _____
9. _____
10. _____
11. _____
12. _____
13. _____
14. _____
15. _____
16. _____
17. _____
18. _____
19. _____
20. _____

SPELLING WORDS

1. charged
2. spied
3. moving
4. trying
5. practicing
6. injured
7. carrying
8. tasted
9. receiving
10. becoming
11. lying
12. dying
13. realized
14. provided
15. fried
16. created
17. tallied
18. carried
19. revising
20. wearing

Practice Book
Distant Voyages

▶ As you read the paragraph, use context clues to determine the meaning of the boldfaced Vocabulary Words. Then match each Vocabulary Word to its definition.

It was the day before the race. Keisha and Annie went over to the race **headquarters** to check in and get their starting **positions.** Keisha and Annie had worked as dog **handlers** for the past three years, so they knew a lot about dogs. They knew how to care for the dogs' feet. They knew when the dogs needed to rest. They also knew how to avoid letting the dogs get into a **tangle.** That would be dangerous and time-consuming. Each racer hoped to keep up a fast **pace** during tomorrow's race.

1. the central office for controlling an operation _____

2. rate of speed _____

3. people who train or manage an animal in a show or contest

_____

4. the places things are, in comparison to other things

_____

5. something that is snarled or muddled

_____

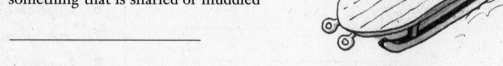

▶ Write the Vocabulary Word that best completes each sentence.

6. The pony show _____ was connected by phone to various offices.

7. The ponies' _____ knew how to prepare the animals for travel.

8. When the ponies perform, they know their correct starting

_____.

9. When several of them pull a wagon, they almost never _____ the reins.

10. Each pony keeps a steady _____ when walking or trotting.

TRY THIS! Write a paragraph about a race you have watched or participated in. Use at least three Vocabulary Words.

© Harcourt

Name _____

▶ **Read the paragraph. Then circle the letter of the best answer to each question.**

The Siberian Husky and the Malamute are the two breeds of dog used most often in Alaska as part of a dogsled team. These dogs are not very large, but they are able to pull heavy sleds over great distances. The most experienced dog is usually put in the forward position as the leader. The dogs need several hours of rest, plus plenty of food and water in order to survive long cross-country trips. With minimal care, a dogsled team will remain strong and eager to run for many hours.

1 What conclusion can you draw about Malamutes and Siberian Huskies based on the paragraph?

A Malamutes are larger than Siberian Huskies.

B Both dogs are very strong.

C The Siberian Husky often has one blue eye and one brown eye.

D They do not make good house pets.

💡 **Tip**

Look for a statement in the paragraph that helps you reach one of the conclusions listed here.

2 Which statement is NOT true?

F Sled dogs will follow a leader.

G All dogs on a team have the same amount of experience.

H Dogs need to rest on a very long run.

J Sled dogs are not large, but they are powerful.

💡 **Tip**

Review the paragraph for a sentence that suggests the opposite of one of these statements.

3 Which generalization best describes Alaskan sled dogs?

A They have a lot of determination.

B They tend to give up after a short time.

C They are friendly and like to be petted.

D They are extremely difficult to train.

💡 **Tip**

What can you conclude about sled dogs, based on the details in the paragraph?

© Harcourt

SCHOOL-HOME CONNECTION Help your child list some equipment that would be needed on a long, cross-country sled trip. Your child should mention equipment for both dogs and people. Discuss the completed list.

33

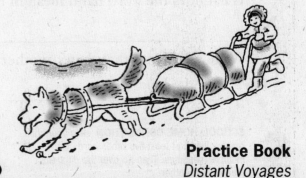

Practice Book
Distant Voyages

▶ **Read the sentences. Then answer the questions.**

1. Good mushers know that keeping dogs calm is the **key** to success. What does the word **key** mean in this sentence?

_____

 Write a sentence that shows another meaning of the word **key**.

_____

2. Moose **tracks** on the trail made the young musher nervous. What does the word **tracks** mean in this sentence?

_____

Write a sentence that shows another meaning of the word **tracks**.

_____

3. When she saw them, her fears began to **mushroom**. What does the word **mushroom** mean in this sentence?

_____

 Write a sentence that shows another meaning of the word **mushroom**.

_____

4. If a moose did appear, all she could hope was that it didn't **charge**. What does the word **charge** mean in this sentence?

_____

Write a sentence that shows another meaning of the word **charge**.

_____

5. When the musher finished the race, everyone gave her a big **hand**. What does the word **hand** mean in this sentence?

_____

Write a sentence that shows another meaning of the word **hand**.

_____

SCHOOL-HOME CONNECTION Help your child
make a list of at least five other words with
multiple meanings. Then go over the different
meanings together.

34

Practice Book
Distant Voyages

© Harcourt

Name _____

Skill Reminder • **A complex sentence** contains an independent clause and at least one dependent clause.
• A dependent clause often begins with a connecting word such as *before, after, because,* or *although.*

▶ Write *complex* or *simple* in the blank following each sentence. For each complex sentence, draw one line under the independent clause and two lines under the dependent clause. Circle the connecting word.

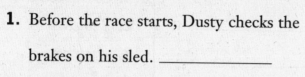

1. Before the race starts, Dusty checks the brakes on his sled. _____

2. Although space is limited, the racers must carry emergency food. _____

3. Each dog looks small but is very strong. _____

4. Because the dogs are so excited, the handlers must hold them. _____

5. The racers take off after the signal to start is given. _____

▶ Rewrite each pair of sentences below to form a complex sentence. Use the connecting word in parentheses to join the parts of the complex sentence.

6. The race starts. Dusty crosses the lake safely. **(after)** _____
_____

7. The dogs enter the woods. Dusty is on edge. **(when)** _____
_____

8. This part of the trail is tricky. It is crowded with obstacles. **(because)** _____
_____

TRY THIS! Experiment with combining simple sentences with different connecting words. What do you notice?

© Harcourt

35

Practice Book
Distant Voyages

Skill Reminder • The unstressed sounds /ən/ can be spelled *an*, *en*, or *on*. • The unstressed sounds /ər/ can be spelled *er* or *or*.

▶ Fold the paper along the dotted line. As each spelling word is read aloud, write it in the blank. Then unfold your paper, and check your work. Practice spelling any words you missed.

1. _____

2. _____

3. _____

4. _____

5. _____

6. _____

7. _____

8. _____

9. _____

10. _____

11. _____

12. _____

13. _____

14. _____

15. _____

16. _____

17. _____

18. _____

19. _____

20. _____

SPELLING WORDS

1. American
2. frozen
3. button
4. chapter
5. tractor
6. golden
7. taken
8. harbor
9. father
10. color
11. ancestor
12. hidden
13. hamburger
14. theater
15. weather
16. beckon
17. cannon
18. comparison
19. elder
20. turban

© Harcourt

Practice Book
Distant Voyages

Name _____

▶ **Write the Vocabulary Word that best completes each sentence.**

| resembled | retired | snort | harness | disengage | bulk | pointedly |

1. Mike's Alaskan husky, Apollo, really _____ a wolf.

2. At Peterson Park, Mike would _____

   Apollo's leash from his _____.

3. With a fierce look, Apollo would _____
   keep other dogs away from his ball.

4. Apollo liked to use his size and _____
   to boss other dogs.

5. His loud _____ made some dogs nervous.

6. Now Mike has _____ Apollo from being
   a harness dog.

▶ **Write a Vocabulary Word to complete each analogy.**

7. *Melt* is to *freeze* as _____ is to *link*.

8. *Almost* is to *exactly* as _____ is to *matched*.

9. *Jeans* is to *denim* as _____ is to *leather*.

10. *Silently* is to *quietly* as _____ is to *noticeably*.

TRY THIS!
Write a paragraph about a dog you know. Use at least three Vocabulary Words in your sentence.

Practice Book
Distant Voyages

Name _____

HOMEWORK

Woodsong

Summarize
and Paraphrase
TEST PREP

▶ **Read the paragraph. Circle the letter of the best answer to each question.**

Everyone who has owned dogs has an abundance of anecdotes about the amazing and amusing things dogs do. Every few months it seems a newspaper article appears about a dog who has rescued a small child from drowning or saved its owners from a fire. Yes, the bond between people and dogs is an intimate one, and it has grown for the thousands of years that people and dogs have lived and worked together.

1 Which is the best summary of the paragraph?

A People and dogs have been closely associated for thousands of years.

B Most people love dogs and have lots of stories to tell about them.

C Dogs have rescued thousands of people over the years.

D Stories about dogs often occur in the newspaper.

> **Tip**
> Choose the answer that pulls together all the ideas in the paragraph.

2 Which is the best paraphrase of the first sentence?

F Dog owners have lots of stories about the amazing and funny things dogs do.

G Everyone who owns dogs likes them.

H People who own dogs complain about their dogs.

J Everyone who has owned dogs tells jokes about the funny things their dogs do.

> **Tip**
> Use context clues to figure out the meaning of *abundance* and *anecdotes.* Then use these meanings to choose the best paraphrase.

3 Which is the best paraphrase of the last sentence?

A Dogs and people have always had a close association.

B Dogs and people have had the same relationship for thousands of years.

C Dogs have been forced to do work for people for thousands of years.

D Dogs and people have grown closer during the thousands of years they have been together.

> **Tip**
> Which answer most completely and accurately states the important point the author makes in the last sentence?

© Harcourt

SCHOOL-HOME CONNECTION Have your child copy a short paragraph from a magazine or newspaper article. Together, write a one- or two-sentence summary of the paragraph. Then paraphrase one of the sentences in the paragraph.

38

Practice Book
Distant Voyages

Name _____

Skill Reminder • A **noun** names a person, a place, a thing, or an idea. Some nouns can be abbreviated. Use a period after most abbreviations. • A **proper noun** names a specific person, place, or thing. Each important word begins with a capital letter. • A **common noun** names any person, place, or thing. It begins with a lowercase letter.

▶ Underline each noun in the sentences below. Write *C* above each common noun and *P* above each proper noun.

1. Gary Paulsen could write a whole book about Storm.

2. The dog had the ears of a bear and was built like a truck.

3. When Storm grew older, he looked like a famous comedian, George Burns.

4. In his fourth year as a puller, he started to play tricks.

▶ Rewrite each sentence. Replace each underlined group of words with a proper noun.

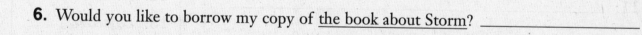

5. The lead dog played jokes on the dog pulling

   next to him. _____

   _____

6. Would you like to borrow my copy of the book about Storm? _____

   _____

7. I would like to meet the author of that book. _____

   _____

▶ Rewrite the sentence. Add punctuation after the abbreviations.

8. Mr Meer climbed Mt Snowcap on Sat, Nov 4. _____

   _____

TRY THIS! Read a short newspaper article. List any proper nouns and abbreviations you notice in the article.

Practice Book
Distant Voyages

© Harcourt

Skill Reminder • The unstressed ending /əl/ can be spelled *el,*
le, al, or *il.*

▶ Fold the paper along the dotted line. As each spelling word is read aloud, write it
in the blank. Then unfold your paper, and check your work. Practice spelling any
words you missed.

1. _____

2. _____

3. _____

4. _____

5. _____

6. _____

7. _____

8. _____

9. _____

10. _____

11. _____

12. _____

13. _____

14. _____

15. _____

16. _____

17. _____

18. _____

19. _____

20. _____

SPELLING WORDS

1. level
2. double
3. metal
4. evil
5. travel
6. couple
7. needle
8. battle
9. candle
10. article
11. equal
12. civil
13. capital
14. original
15. individual
16. material
17. angel
18. camel
19. illegal
20. stencil

Practice Book
Distant Voyages

Name _____

▶ **As you read the paragraphs, use context clues to determine the meaning of the boldfaced Vocabulary Words. Then write the correct Vocabulary Word next to its definition.**

Lee Ann and John were going diving in the ocean. Though their dog, Peaches, gave them a **forlorn** look, they left her home because she would hate being on a boat all day. Lee Ann wore an old T-shirt and suit, but since John was **vainer** than Lee Ann, he wore his new trunks and matching mask and fins.

Their boat **pitched** on the rough sea, but underwater all was calm. Lee Ann and John saw many marvelous sights diving—even the **lair** of an eel. When they found shells of their favorite sea creature, **abalone,** they were just about **overcome** with joy.

Back on land at the end of the day, Lee Ann and John were so hungry they **gorged** themselves at dinner. They went to sleep early and dreamed of the ocean.

1. plunged and rose again and again _____

2. feeling miserable, lost, or abandoned _____

3. more involved in one's own appearance
   than others are _____

4. overwhelmed; taken over _____

5. overate; gobbled like an animal _____

6. the home of some kinds of animals _____

7. a water animal that lives in a shell _____

▶ **Write the Vocabulary Word that best completes each sentence.**

8. John was _____ by tiredness after he ate.

9. Lee Ann had a _____ look as she said good-bye.

10. She took the shell of an _____ with her.

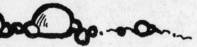

TRY THIS! Write a paragraph about a tropical island, real or made up. Tell what the island looks like and what someone might discover there. Use at least four Vocabulary Words in your sentences.

© Harcourt

Name _____

▶ **Read the paragraph. Then circle the letter of the best answer to each question.**

    Annie and Sara loved to take long hikes over the hills on their island. Sometimes they talked and laughed as they walked, but often they just listened to the wind and the chirps of birds. The girls were hiking silently early Sunday morning when they heard a small noise. They followed the sound off the trail, and it grew louder. On a tree branch overhanging a pond, they saw a small cat hanging on for dear life. Talking to it gently so as not to frighten it, Sara slowly leaned over and freed the cat. Annie prepared a soft place for it in her backpack.

1 What do you know about Annie and Sara?

  A They do not get along well.

  B They are afraid of animals.

  C They are friends.

  D They live in a flat, dry area.

 Tip
What sense do you get about the girls from the first few sentences?

2 What problem do the characters face?

  F Only one of them has a backpack.

  G A noise is disturbing their hike.

  H They walk off the path and get lost.

  J They find a frightened cat.

Tip
Think about the most serious thing that happens to the girls.

3 What must be done before the problem can be resolved?

  A Sara must calm the cat down.

  B Sara must climb the tree.

  C Annie must find her backpack.

  D The girls must get over their fear.

Tip
First find the solution; then work backward from it to answer this question.

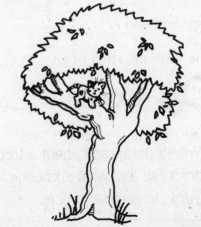

© Harcourt

SCHOOL-HOME CONNECTION What will Annie and Sara do next? Work with your child to continue the story.

Practice Book
Distant Voyages

Name _____

▶ **Read each passage. Then answer each question.**

Binh's stomach fluttered. She went over the list of supplies in her mind: matches, sleeping bag, plastic sheet, knife, hatchet, and all the rest. Her adventure was going to start soon, whether she was ready or not.

1. How is Binh feeling right now? _____

_____

2. What words and phrases helped you make this inference? _____

_____

After three days in the wilderness, Binh set up her tent and made a fire in half the time it had taken her at first. She ate a good dinner of freeze-dried stew and freshly picked berries, played the harmonica for a while, and fell asleep the instant she stretched out in her sleeping bag.

3. How does Binh feel about wilderness camping after three days? _____

_____

4. What words and phrases helped you make this inference? _____

_____

The entire class was absolutely silent as Binh gave her report, their eyes fixed on her face. When Binh told about her run-in with the fox, you could hear a huge gasp as everyone drew in their breath at the same time.

5. Was the class puzzled, bored, or fascinated by Binh's report? _____

_____

6. What words and phrases helped you make this inference? _____

_____

© Harcourt

SCHOOL-HOME CONNECTION With your child, make a list of ten things to take to a desert island. Ask your child to give a reason for each of his or her choices and to make inferences about your reasons for the choices you added to the list.

Practice Book
Distant Voyages

Name _____

Skill Reminder • A **singular noun** names one person, place,
thing, or idea. A **plural noun** names more than one person,
place, thing, or idea.   • **Regular nouns** become plural if you add *-s* or *-es*.
Change the y at the end of some regular nouns to *i* before adding *-es*.
• Some **irregular nouns** have a special spelling in the plural form. Others
have the same spelling for both the singular and plural forms.

▶ Write the nouns in each sentence on the line. Write *singular* or *plural* after
each noun.

1. The wind blew in fierce gusts. _____

2. It stung our faces. _____

3. My brother carried our baskets. _____

4. We were hoping to catch many fish. _____

5. Four men stood beside the boats. _____

▶ Rewrite each sentence, using the plural of the noun in parentheses.

6. Sometimes the people had (**party**) on the beach. _____

_____

7. The (**child**) would play in the water. _____

_____

8. All the (**guest**) ate the tasty (**fish**). _____

_____

© Harcourt

44

Skill Reminder • To form the plural of most words, add -s
or -es. • For words ending in a consonant and y, change y to i
and add -es. • For some words, change the final *f* or *fe* to v and add -es.
• For some words from Latin, change -is to -es or change -um to -a

▶ Fold the paper along the dotted line. As each spelling word is read aloud, write it
in the blank. Then unfold your paper, and check your work. Practice spelling any
words you missed.

1. _____

2. _____

3. _____

4. _____

5. _____

6. _____

7. _____

8. _____

9. _____

10. _____

11. _____

12. _____

13. _____

14. _____

15. _____

16. _____

17. _____

18. _____

19. _____

20. _____

SPELLING WORDS

1. crises
2. knives
3. media
4. roofs
5. pianos
6. waves
7. wishes
8. armies
9. briefs
10. videos
11. heroes
12. data
13. bacteria
14. oxen
15. tomatoes
16. canoes
17. berries
18. loaves
19. lives
20. messages

Practice Book
Distant Voyages

Name _____

▶ Read each sentence, using context clues to determine the meaning of the boldfaced Vocabulary Word. Then write each Vocabulary Word after its definition.

There was a **plenitude** of plant life in the rainforest.

A **multitude** of birds flew overhead.

Small animals **scurried** on the jungle floor.

We wondered what it was like **eons** ago, when Earth was young.

We sat down and **pondered** what to explore next.

That's when I noticed we were on a **peninsula**, not an island.

1. ample amount; abundance _____

2. ran lightly; scampered _____

3. longest divisions of geologic time _____

4. land surrounded by water on three sides _____

5. a very great number _____

6. weighed carefully in the mind _____

▶ Follow the directions below.

7. Write a sentence about Earth when dinosaurs existed. Use the Vocabulary Word **eons** in your sentence.

_____

_____

8. Write a sentence about an experience you had exploring the natural world. Use the word **plenitude** in your sentence.

_____

_____

Write a short story that takes place *eons* ago. Use your Vocabulary Words.

Practice Book
Distant Voyages

© Harcourt

Name _____

▶ **Read the paragraph. Then circle the letter of the best answer to each question.**

    A small fishing boat transported us to the island. "Be careful, and be sure to be back at the dock at four o'clock," the captain said as he dropped us off. We had a fascinating day exploring the lush island with its multitude of wild animals. Late in the afternoon, Danny had the <u>misfortune</u> of twisting his ankle. He moved so slowly and painfully, I thought it would be <u>impossible</u> to reach the dock by four o'clock, but we made it. In a few days Danny's ankle had healed. We couldn't stop talking about our <u>wonderful</u> trip.

1 What does the word *wonderful* mean?

  A full of wonder

  B without wonder

  C needing wonder

  D the act of wondering

> 💡 **Tip**
> What is the root of the word *wonderful*? What meaning does the suffix *-ful* add?

2 What is the root of the word *misfortune*?

  A for

  B fortune

  C mis

  D fortunate

> 💡 **Tip**
> Remove the prefix. What word is left?

3 Which word does NOT have the same prefix as the word *impossible*?

  A immovable

  B image

  C impolite

  D imbalance

> 💡 **Tip**
> Think of the meaning of *im-* in the word *impossible*, and compare it to the meaning of *im-* in the answer choices.

© Harcourt

SCHOOL-HOME CONNECTION With your child, make a list of words that have the prefixes *im-* and *mis-* or the suffix *-ful.* Then use each word in a sentence.

47

Name _____

▶ **Read each question. Then write the keywords that you would use to search the Internet for the answer. Use quotation marks (" ") at the beginning and end of a phrase if you want the whole phrase to be part of your search.**

1. Are Florida's Everglades classified as a national park?

_____ AND _____

2. How has development affected the wildlife of the Everglades?

_____ AND _____ AND _____

3. What is the most unusual plant that grows in the Everglades?

_____

4. Where is a good place to stay for visitors of the Everglades?

_____

5. Which Native Americans live near the Everglades?

_____ AND _____

▶ **Answer the questions about using a card catalog.**

6. What type of card would you look for to see whether a library has a book on the Everglades?

_____

7. What two types of cards would you use to find a book by William Thompson about the Everglades?

_____

8. Which title comes first in the card catalog? Why? *Animals of the Everglades, Birds of the Everglades, An Adventure in the Everglades.*

_____

_____

SCHOOL-HOME CONNECTION Help your child do an Internet search at your local library. Research a topic that interests him or her, using keywords.

48

Practice Book
Distant Voyages

© Harcourt

Skill Reminder • **A possessive noun** shows ownership.
• To form the possessive of most singular nouns, add an apostrophe and the letter *s* ('s). • To form the possessive of a plural noun that ends in the letter *s*, add only an apostrophe ('). • To form the possessive of a plural noun that does not end in the letter *s*, add an apostrophe and the letter *s* ('s).

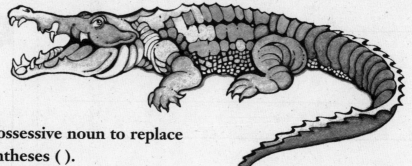

▶ Write a singular possessive noun to replace each word in parentheses ( ).

1. (Shaneesha) _____ voice sounded excited.

2. "The (alligator) _____ mouth had millions of small pointy teeth," she told her friend Denice.

3. Her (friend) _____ eyes grew wide.

4. Denice marveled, "You would have been bitten if the (mangrove)

_____ low branches hadn't saved you!"

▶ Write a plural possessive noun to replace each word in parentheses ( ).

5. "All mangrove (tree) _____ branches are low," Shaneesha reassured Denice.

6. Shaneesha explained that she had been more frightened of the (paths)

_____ twists and turns than she had been of the animals.

7. Shaneesha hadn't liked the (swamps) _____ insects.

8. (Women) _____ voices singing in the distance calmed her down.

TRY THIS! Write six sentences about things your friends or family members own. Use singular possessive nouns in three of the sentences and plural possessive nouns in the other three.

49

Practice Book
Distant Voyages

Name _____

Skill Reminder • "Silent" letters are often found in these
consonant pairs: *sl (s); gn (g); lm, lf, lk (l); mn (n); wr, sw (w).*

▶ Fold the paper along the dotted line. As each spelling word is read aloud, write it
in the blank. Then unfold your paper, and check your work. Practice spelling any
words you missed.

1. _____
2. _____
3. _____
4. _____
5. _____
6. _____
7. _____
8. _____
9. _____
10. _____
11. _____
12. _____
13. _____
14. _____
15. _____
16. _____
17. _____
18. _____
19. _____
20. _____

SPELLING WORDS

1. island
2. design
3. calm
4. column
5. sword
6. half
7. yolk
8. walked
9. talk
10. chalk
11. wrinkled
12. wrong
13. autumn
14. solemn
15. aisle
16. foreign
17. lightning
18. benign
19. glistened
20. resign

© Harcourt

Practice Book
Distant Voyages

Name _____

▶ As you read the paragraph, use context clues to determine the meaning of each boldfaced Vocabulary Word. Then write each Vocabulary Word next to its definition.

In the park, water supplies had **dwindled** to a fifty-year low. It seemed as if the spray from the **geyser** was the only source of water around. Every camper tried to follow the **policy** of drenching his or her campfire to make sure that no **embers** remained lighted. A forest fire started anyway, though, because lightning ignited the brush, which was dry as **tinder**. The resulting fire soon burned small trees and the leaves and branches in the **canopy** above. When the wind shifted, the fire **veered** first one way and then the other.

1. underground water that is naturally heated and then

shoots out from the ground _____

2. dry twigs and leaves that easily catch fire _____

3. turned sharply from a straight direction _____

4. in a fire, glowing pieces of wood _____

5. a rooflike covering _____

6. shrank in size, value, or quantity _____

7. the set of rules of an organization _____

▶ Write the Vocabulary Word that best completes each sentence.

8. We watched the _____ shoot steam into the air.

9. As we hiked, our water supply _____.

10. Under the ash, _____ still glowed.

 TRY THIS! Write three sentences that describe a *canopy*. Use descriptive words to tell how it looks, feels, or sounds.

Practice Book
Distant Voyages

Name _____

▶ **Read the paragraph. Look at the map. Then circle the letter of the best answer to each question.**

Yellowstone National Park has more than 2 million acres. Visitors to the park enjoy seeing the Grand Canyon of Yellowstone, the geyser called Old Faithful, and Yellowstone Lake. Year round, visitors can see bison. The bison graze in the meadows between Old Faithful and Madison.

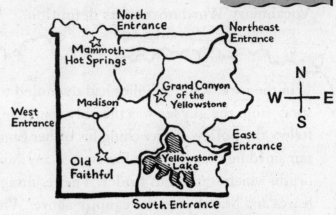

Yellowstone National Park

1 What information in the passage does the map help you understand?

  A the location of bison in the park

  B the size of the park

  C the depth of the Grand Canyon of Yellowstone

  D how Old Faithful looks

 Tip

Think about information that is in both the passage and the map. Decide which information the map helps you understand.

2 Which of the following is directly north of Yellowstone Lake?

  F Madison

  G Old Faithful

  H Grand Canyon of Yellowstone

  J Mammoth Hot Springs

Tip

Find Yellowstone Lake on the map. The compass rose will help you find the spot that is north of the lake.

3 Which of the following do you learn from the map, but not from the passage?

  A that Old Faithful is in Yellowstone Park

  B the number of bison in the park

  C that bison can be seen all year

  D that bison are found on the west side of the park

Tip

Look for information found only on the map. Remember, a map usually helps you visualize location.

© Harcourt

SCHOOL-HOME CONNECTION With your child, draw a map of your home or neighborhood. Have your child mark and label important places. Be sure to show where north is on the map.

52

Practice Book
Distant Voyages

Name _____

▶ **Read the paragraphs. Then answer the questions.**

The Yellowstone Fires

On May 24, 1988, the fire season in Yellowstone began when lightning struck a tree in the northeastern part of the park. On June 23, lightning started another fire, in the southern part of the park. Two days later, another bolt of lightning started a fire, in the northwestern section of the park. Nobody tried to put out these fires because the summer rains were expected to begin soon.

Unexpected Problems

That summer, however, the rains did not come. By mid-July, 8,600 acres of forest had burned. Throughout July and August, the fires grew, jumping rivers, roads, canyons, and parking lots. By August 20, more than 150,000 acres had burned. By September 6, fire fighters had moved in to defend the area around Old Faithful. The fire that was threatening the geyser had started on July 22 and had grown since then.

Unexpected Relief

At the last moment, on September 7, the wind shifted, and the fire turned away from Old Faithful. Finally, on September 10, rain began falling. The next day, snow began to fall. Scattered fires continued to burn until November, but the worst was over.

1. In what kind of text structure are events told in the order they happened?

_____

2. Which subhead tells you about how things got better? _____

▶ **Fill in the blanks with what happened on each date shown on the time line.**

May 24, 1988 — **3.** _____

4. _____

June 23, 1988
June 25, 1988 — **5.** _____

6. _____

July 22, 1988 — **7.** _____

8. _____

9. _____

September 6, 1988
September 7, 1988 —
September 10, 1988 — **10.** _____
September 11, 1988

Name _____

Skill Reminder • A **pronoun** is a word that takes the place of
one or more nouns. • Pronouns show number and gender.
Number tells whether a pronoun is singular or plural. **Gender** tells whether
the pronoun is masculine, feminine, or neuter. • The **antecedent** is the
noun or nouns to which the pronoun refers.

▶ Write a pronoun to replace the word or words in parentheses ( ).

1. Lightning struck suddenly, and **(the lightning)** _____
quickly caused fire to break out.

2. Animals roamed the parks, and **(the animals)** _____
might be in danger.

3. Two fire fighters came too close, and the fire almost burned

(the fire fighters) _____ .

4. Fire crews knew that **(the fire crews)** _____ could not
control the raging fires.

5. On smoky days, the sun was so dim that **(the sun)** _____
looked like the moon.

▶ Rewrite each sentence, replacing the underlined word or words with a pronoun.

6. Mark, a fire fighter, looked at the buildings near Old Faithful, and Mark was worried.

_____

7. Of the eight major fires burning in Yellowstone Park, one of the fires was moving

toward the geyser. _____

_____

8. The fire almost reached the inn, but a shift in the wind kept the fire away from Old

Faithful. _____

_____

**TRY
THIS!** Write five sentences about a natural event such as a fire or storm. Use as many
nouns and pronouns as possible. Then identify each pronoun and the word it
refers to.

Name _____

Skill Reminder • **A compound word is made by combining two or more smaller words. The spelling of these smaller words remains the same.** • **Some compound words are written as one word, some are written as two words, and some are hyphenated.**

▶ Fold the paper along the dotted line. As each spelling word is read aloud, write it in the blank. Then unfold your paper, and check your work. Practice spelling any words you missed.

1. _____

2. _____

3. _____

4. _____

5. _____

6. _____

7. _____

8. _____

9. _____

10. _____

11. _____

12. _____

13. _____

14. _____

15. _____

16. _____

17. _____

18. _____

19. _____

20. _____

SPELLING WORDS

1. basketball
2. seventy-five
3. rock band
4. everybody
5. fireplace
6. anything
7. take-off
8. skateboard
9. homework
10. two-thirds
11. high school
12. railroad
13. motorcycle
14. vice president
15. strawberry
16. freeway
17. car pool
18. comic strip
19. fine arts
20. forty-two

Practice Book
Distant Voyages

© Harcourt

55

Name _____

▶ **Read the Vocabulary Words. Then write the Vocabulary Word that best completes each sentence.**

bulge	energy	generated
gravitational	shallow	inlet

1. The _____ pull of the moon and the sun affects the daily tides.

2. The high tide created a _____ in the ocean water.

3. During low tide, the water can be so _____ the muddy bottom can be seen.

4. The boats were anchored in a narrow _____ near the island.

5. In the past, underwater earthquakes have _____ damaging waves.

6. People have often wondered how to use the _____ of waves.

▶ **Write the Vocabulary Word with the opposite meaning of each word or phrase.**

7. sunken area _____

8. deep _____

9. destroyed _____

 TRY THIS! Write a paragraph about an underwater earthquake. Use all of your Vocabulary Words.

© Harcourt

Name _____

HOMEWORK

Oceans

Text Structure:
Main Idea
and Details
TEST PREP

▶ **Read the passage. Then circle the letter of the best answer to each question.**

   People have used various methods to measure the depth of the ocean. Long ago sailors lowered a rope over the side of the ship. When the end of the rope touched bottom, they knew how deep the water was. Today scientists measure the depth of the water with an echo sounder. It bounces sound waves off the bottom of the ocean. The depth of the ocean is determined by the amount of time it takes the sound waves to travel.

1 What is the main idea of this passage?

   A Ropes measure the depth of the ocean.

   B Echo sounders measure the depth of the ocean.

   C Sailors measure the depth of the ocean.

   D Different methods have been used to measure the depth of the ocean.

> 💡 **Tip**
> Find the sentence in the paragraph that summarizes the passage.

2 How is this passage organized?

   F The main idea is first. The details follow.

   G The main idea is in the middle. The details are first and last.

   H The details are first. The main idea is last.

   J There are only details.

> 💡 **Tip**
> Think about the kinds of sentences that follow the main idea.

3 Which of the following is a detail in this passage?

   A Various methods have been used to measure the ocean's depth.

   B Sailors sail on ships.

   C Echo sounders bounce sound waves off the bottom of the ocean.

   D Diving can take sailors into deep water.

> 💡 **Tip**
> Look back at the passage. Find the answer choice that is a detail.

© Harcourt

SCHOOL-HOME CONNECTION Search through a newspaper or magazine with your child. Read an article together and determine its main idea. Then ask your child to find details in the article that support it.

57

Practice Book
Distant Voyages

Name _____

Skill Reminder • **Subject pronouns** take the place of a noun or nouns in the subject. *I, you, he, she, it, we,* and *they* are subject pronouns. • **Object pronouns** take the place of a noun after an action verb or a preposition. *Me, you, him, her, it, us,* and *them* are object pronouns.

▶ Write a subject pronoun to replace the word or words in parentheses ( ).

1. (Kevin) _____ knows what causes tides.

2. (Mrs. Farnham) _____ had explained the process.

3. (Tides) _____ are the result of gravitational pull.

▶ Write an object pronoun to replace the word or words in parentheses ( ).

4. Spring tides occur when the combined pull of the sun

and the moon produce (**spring tides**) _____.

5. The ocean water in a wave does not move along

with (**the wave**) _____.

6. Marie helped Kevin by drawing a wave diagram

for (**Kevin**) _____.

▶ Rewrite each sentence with a subject or an object pronoun that fits in each blank.

7. The land is affected by the water surrounding _____.

_____

_____

8. _____ took photographs of beach erosion. _____

_____

9. Marvin and I collected rocks, and _____ saw that _____ were worn smooth by the

waves. _____

_____

© Harcourt

Practice Book
Distant Voyages

Name _____

Skill Reminder Words and phrases that sound similar will not be troublesome if you remember which spelling goes with which usage.

▶ Fold the paper along the dotted line. As each spelling word is read aloud, write it in the blank. Then unfold your paper, and check your work. Practice spelling any words you missed.

1. _____
2. _____
3. _____
4. _____
5. _____
6. _____
7. _____
8. _____
9. _____
10. _____
11. _____
12. _____
13. _____
14. _____
15. _____
16. _____
17. _____
18. _____
19. _____
20. _____

SPELLING WORDS

1. anyway
2. any way
3. all right
4. every one
5. everyone
6. already
7. all ready
8. a lot
9. its
10. it's
11. your
12. you're
13. who's
14. whose
15. there's
16. theirs
17. anyone
18. any one
19. altogether
20. all together

© Harcourt

59

Name _____

▶ **Read the Vocabulary Words. Then read the groups of related words. Write the Vocabulary Word that belongs in each group.**

| sensors | lagoon | meander | reef | atoll | barren |

1. island
peninsula
continent

_____

2. lake
pond
ocean

_____

3. coral
sand
ridge

_____

4. detectors
monitors
electronics

_____

5. empty
lifeless
bare

_____

6. wind
twist
turn

_____

▶ **Write the Vocabulary Word that best completes each sentence.**

The **(7)** _____ was formed when the volcano sank into the ocean.

The ring of land was formed by a coral **(8)** _____. The center of this

kind of island is a **(9)** _____. People sometimes **(10)** _____

around islands like this. They use **(11)** _____ to look for metal objects

under the ground. Usually, the islands are **(12)** _____, with little or

nothing on them.

TRY THIS! Write a paragraph about a visit to another planet. Include these Vocabulary Words in your paragraph: *meander, barren, sensors, lagoon.*

© Harcourt

60

Practice Book
Distant Voyages

Name _____

▶ **Read the paragraph. Look at the diagram. Circle the letter of the best answer to each question.**

Volcanoes are reminders that the Earth is always changing. Volcanoes can help to support life. In the waters of the South Seas, the submerged sides of volcanoes support corals, which form coral reefs. Volcanoes can also endanger life. If a volcano erupts, hot lava and ash spew out. A river of hot lava may then flow down the sides of the mountain, destroying everything in its path—plants, animals, buildings, and people. Volcanoes show the power of nature.

volcano

ash and lava

layers of rock

molten rock, or magma

An Erupting Volcano

1 Which part of the passage does the diagram clarify?

A that volcanoes remind us that the Earth is changing

B how the submerged sides of volcanoes support corals

C how hot lava and ash spew out of erupting volcanoes

D that a river of hot lava can destroy animals and people

> 💡 **Tip**
> Read the title and labels on the diagram.

2 Which of the following do you learn about from the diagram but not from the passage?

F the formation of a coral reef

G the inside of a volcano

H the powerful nature of a volcano

J the value of volcanoes

> 💡 **Tip**
> Which answer choice is <u>not</u> covered in the passage?

© Harcourt

SCHOOL-HOME CONNECTION Work with your child to make a diagram of something he or she uses daily in your home. Label the important parts.

61

Name _____

▶ **Read the list of facts on these two index cards. Then answer the questions.**

a. *The Viking satellite photographed Mars.*

b. *The average temperature on Mars is much colder than on Earth.*

c. *A round trip from Earth to Mars could take from two to three years.*

from *Pioneering Space* by Sandra Markle, N.Y., Atheneum, 1992.

d. *In 1976 two space probes, Viking landers, touched down on Mars.*

e. *Two spacecraft launched in 1996 continue to study Mars from orbit and from the surface.*

f. *Mars has dust storms strong enough to bury a space probe.*

from *Space Exploration* by Carol Stott. NY: Alfred K. Knopf, 1997.

1. What three facts would you use to write about the difficulty astronauts might have exploring Mars? Write them on the lines.

_____

_____

_____

2. Write a specific conclusion that you can draw from these three facts. _____

_____

3. What three facts would you use to tell how scientists have learned about Mars? Write them on the lines.

_____

_____

_____

4. Write a specific conclusion you can draw from these three facts. _____

_____

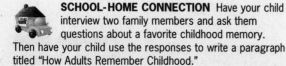

SCHOOL-HOME CONNECTION Have your child interview two family members and ask them questions about a favorite childhood memory. Then have your child use the responses to write a paragraph titled "How Adults Remember Childhood."

62

Practice Book
Distant Voyages

© Harcourt

Name _____

Skill Reminder • **Possessive pronouns** show ownership and take the place of a noun. The possessive pronouns *my, our, your, his, her, its,* and *their* are used before nouns. The possessive pronouns *mine, ours, yours, his, hers, its,* and *theirs* stand alone.

▶ **Choose the correct possessive pronoun from the two choices in parentheses ( ). Write it on the line.**

1. Patricia Lauber was inspired to write "Seeing Earth from Space" by _____ fascination with images of Earth as seen from space. **(her, hers)**

2. Frank Borman was an astronaut, and _____ spacecraft was the *Apollo 8.* **(his, its)**

3. _____ fellow astronauts were James A. Lovell, Jr., and William A. Anders. **(His, Her)**

4. The photographs they took of Earth give us a different view of _____ planet. **(our, ours)**

5. When they see Earth from space, astronauts are amazed at _____ beauty. **(their, its)**

▶ **Underline the incorrect possessive pronoun in each sentence. Then rewrite each sentence correctly on the lines below.**

6. Earth belongs to all of us. It is our.

_____

7. The responsibility for Earth is your as well as mine.

_____

8. All people must do theirs part to protect our planet.

_____

Practice Book
Distant Voyages

© Harcourt

Name _____

Skill Reminder • **There are no rules that tell whether to use** *-ant* **or** *-ent.* **Sometimes it helps to think of the spelling of a related word—for example,** *absence/absent, instance/instant.*

▶ Fold the paper along the dotted line. As each spelling word is read aloud, write it in the blank. Then unfold your paper, and check your work. Practice spelling any words you missed.

1. _____

2. _____

3. _____

4. _____

5. _____

6. _____

7. _____

8. _____

9. _____

10. _____

11. _____

12. _____

13. _____

14. _____

15. _____

16. _____

17. _____

18. _____

19. _____

20. _____

SPELLING WORDS

1. absent
2. servant
3. present
4. instant
5. accident
6. assistant
7. current
8. moment
9. resident
10. ignorant
11. pleasant
12. distant
13. innocent
14. intelligent
15. restaurant
16. patient
17. government
18. statement
19. migrant
20. participant

© Harcourt

Practice Book
Distant Voyages

Name _____

▶ **Read the Vocabulary Words. Then write the Vocabulary Word that best completes each sentence.**

translation	publicity	features	piercing	advanced

We couldn't understand a word the creatures said, so we turned to our trusty

(1) _____ machine for help. All of the creatures had

(2) _____ eyes that seemed to penetrate into our thoughts.

Their other **(3)** _____, especially their mouths, seemed very small.

Soon it became clear that they wanted to brag about how **(4)** _____
their civilization was. They had even printed up advertising flyers to get themselves a

little free **(5)** _____!

▶ **Write the Vocabulary Word that best fits with each group of words.**

mouth
ears
nose
chin

newspaper
radio
flyers
announcements

6. _____

7. _____

civilized
smart
ahead
cultured

8. _____

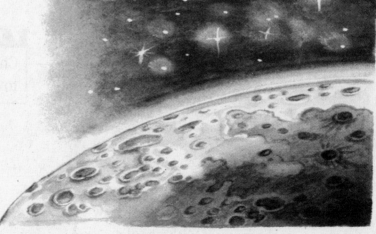

 TRY THIS! Write the first paragraph of a science-fiction story. Use at least three Vocabulary Words in your paragraph.

65

Name _____

▶ **Read the paragraph. Then circle the letter of the best answer to each question.**

Many books contain accounts of UFO sightings and close encounters with extraterrestrials, or creatures from other planets. People have even described being taken to other planets and returning home safely. It seems that for some people, the idea of aliens from other planets is appealing. Many years of alleged sightings have raised unanswered questions. Until proof is provided, we must assume that extraterrestrial life does not exist.

1 What is the main idea of this paragraph?

  A People claim to have been taken to other planets.

  B Many people have seen aliens.

  C There is no proof that extraterrestrial life exists.

  D Many books contain accounts of UFO sightings.

💡 **Tip**

Which answer choice best expresses the author's important ideas and feelings about the topic?

2 Which detail supports this main idea?

  F People have described returning home safely.

  G The idea of aliens is appealing.

  H Proof of aliens has raised questions.

  J Years of alleged sightings have not provided answers.

💡 **Tip**

Which answer choice gives more information about the author's opinion?

3 Which of these details could also be used to support the main idea?

  A Roswell, New Mexico is a well-known UFO center.

  B Weather balloons have sometimes been mistaken for flying saucers.

  C TV shows like *The X-Files* show how aliens might interact with people.

  D People often fear what they do not know.

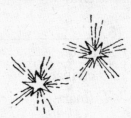

💡 **Tip**

Choose the detail that could be used to show why there is no "firm proof."

SCHOOL-HOME CONNECTION Have your child read several paragraphs from a textbook and identify the main ideas. Which main ideas are stated? Which have to be figured out from the details the writer includes?

Practice Book
Distant Voyages

© Harcourt

Name _____

▶ **Look at the pictures. Then answer the questions below.**

1. How does the alien feel about the dog?

_____

2. How does the dog feel about the alien? _____

3. Suppose this was a photo in a newspaper. On whom would the newspaper focus if it wanted to show that aliens are curious about dogs?

_____

4. From the evidence in the picture, what will probably happen next?

_____

5. How do the alien and the dog feel about each other now?

_____

6. If you were a newspaper reporter, how would you write the first sentence in this story, based on the picture?

_____

SCHOOL-HOME CONNECTION With your child, listen to the lead story on the news. How does the reporter want you to feel about the story? What words or images are used to convey this message?

Practice Book
Distant Voyages

© Harcourt

Name _____

Skill Reminder • The **case** of a pronoun is the form that shows how it is used in a sentence. • A subject pronoun is in the **subjective case**. • An object pronoun is in the **objective case**. • A possessive pronoun is in the **possessive case**.

▶ In the sentences below, underline the subject pronouns once. Underline the object pronouns twice. Circle the possessive pronouns.

1. Dan and I heard a strange noise coming from my bedroom ceiling.

2. He said that something must be drilling through our roof.

3. We saw something that startled him more than me.

4. Aliens were coming to visit us.

5. They smiled, and their skin seemed to glow.

▶ Write the kind of sentence asked for in each question.

6. Write the sentence that has a pronoun in the objective case.

   A She loves to read books about aliens.

   B *Weird Stories* is her favorite book.

   C The author, Dan Salvage, wrote a letter to her.

   _____

7. Write the sentence that has a pronoun in the subjective case.

   A Mr. Salvage thanked her for writing.

   B His letter was fascinating to read.

   C He must have spent a lot of time on that letter.

   _____

8. Write the sentence that has a pronoun in the possessive case.

   A She and Dad were so excited!

   B Her dad read the letter and wanted to read the book.

   C "Give it to me," he said.

   _____

Name _____

Skill Reminder • **When you add the suffix _-tion_ to a word, the spelling of the base word changes if it ends in silent e.** • **When you add the suffix _-ness_, the spelling of the base word changes if it ends in y.**

▶ Fold the paper along the dotted line. As each spelling word is read aloud, write it in the blank. Then unfold your paper, and check your work. Practice spelling any words you missed.

1. _____

2. _____

3. _____

4. _____

5. _____

6. _____

7. _____

8. _____

9. _____

10. _____

11. _____

12. _____

13. _____

14. _____

15. _____

16. _____

17. _____

18. _____

19. _____

20. _____

SPELLING WORDS

1. translation
2. laziness
3. population
4. invention
5. generation
6. examination
7. situation
8. operation
9. sickness
10. kindness
11. closeness
12. forgiveness
13. pollution
14. imagination
15. education
16. transportation
17. federation
18. subtraction
19. smallness
20. lateness

Practice Book
Distant Voyages

▶ **Read the Vocabulary Words. Then write the Vocabulary Word that best completes each sentence.**

rations	**despair**	**concocted**
brooded	**homestead**	**undeniable**
perch		

1. The idea that pioneer life would be difficult was _____.

2. Still, it was a good opportunity to _____ and build something for the future.

3. The year the crops failed, there were small _____ of flour and meat.

4. The settlers could not give in to _____, for they had to keep on going.

5. From its _____, a little bird sang a happy song.

6. The farmer had _____ over his difficulties for days, but the bird's song made him feel better.

7. He _____ a plan that he thought would work.

▶ **Write the Vocabulary Word that best completes each analogy.**

8. *Joy* is to *sorrow* as *hope* is to _____.

9. *Recipe* is to *created* as *invention* is to _____.

10. *Spend* is to *money* as *conserve* is to _____.

11. *Person* is to *chair* as *bird* is to _____.

12. *Lie* is to *doubtful* as *truth* is to _____.

TRY THIS! Find another definition of *perch*. Write and illustrate a sentence for each meaning of the word.

Name _____

▶ **Read the paragraph. Use context clues to help determine the meaning of the underlined words. Then circle the letter of the best answer to each question.**

It is early morning, and the fog is still swirling around the surface of the lake. Several fishermen <u>perch</u> on the seats of their boats looking for movement on the water. One of the anglers gets lucky, and he feels a tug on his line. A <u>bass</u> has swallowed the bait. He sets the hook and begins to reel in the line. The bass begins to struggle. Will the fisherman <u>land</u> the bass, or will it get away?

1 What does the word *perch* mean in this paragraph?

  A a type of fish

  B a stand for a bird

  C to sit atop something

  D a covered outdoor space attached to a house

> **Tip**
> Look at how the word *perch* is used. Figuring out what part of speech *perch* is in the sentence will help you choose the correct meaning.

2 What meaning does *reel* have in this paragraph?

  F actual or true

  G a kind of lively dance

  H a kind of gold coin

  J to pull in by winding

> **Tip**
> Notice how *reel* is spelled in the paragraph. Which answer choices can you eliminate right away because they are definitions for *real*?

3 What does *land* mean in this paragraph?

  A catch

  B come down from the air

  C solid part of the earth's surface

  D ground or soil

> **Tip**
> What part of speech is *land* in this sentence? Which definition makes sense when writing about catching a bass?

SCHOOL-HOME CONNECTION Discuss with your child the different meanings and pronunciations that the words *desert, perfect,* and *object* can have.

71

Practice Book
Distant Voyages

© Harcourt

Name _____

Skill Reminder • **A reflexive pronoun refers back to the subject of a sentence.** • **Reflexive pronouns are formed by adding *-self* or *-selves* to certain pronouns. *Myself, yourself, himself, herself,* and *itself* are singular forms. *Ourselves, yourselves,* and *themselves* are plural forms.**

▶ Underline the reflexive pronoun in each sentence. In the blank, write whether the pronoun is *singular* or *plural*. Then circle the word to which the pronoun refers.

1. Momma prepared herself for the party.   _____

2. Eddie made a big sign all by himself.   _____

3. I sat myself down near Grandaddy.   _____

4. The guests were enjoying themselves.   _____

▶ Rewrite each sentence, using the correct pronoun of the two in parentheses ( ).

5. Hattie promised **(yourself, herself)** that she would go to Nebraska.

_____

6. She and Otto prepared **(ourselves, themselves)** for the long journey.

_____

7. Hattie was celebrating **(her, herself)** sixteenth birthday.

_____

8. Grandaddy told **(myself, himself)** that he might never see Hattie again.

_____

TRY THIS! Which reflexive pronoun should be used with each subject in this sentence? (*She, He, The dog, The twins, We*) could see _____ in the mirror.

Practice Book
Distant Voyages

Name _____

Skill Reminder • The spelling of the base word may change when the suffix *-able* is added. • The suffix *-less* means "without." • The suffix *-able* usually means "capable of being."

▶ Fold the paper along the dotted line. As each spelling word is read aloud, write it in the blank. Then unfold your paper, and check your work. Practice spelling any words you missed.

1. _____

2. _____

3. _____

4. _____

5. _____

6. _____

7. _____

8. _____

9. _____

10. _____

11. _____

12. _____

13. _____

14. _____

15. _____

16. _____

17. _____

18. _____

19. _____

20. _____

SPELLING WORDS

1. capable
2. careless
3. desirable
4. admirable
5. restless
6. available
7. debatable
8. tasteless
9. helpless
10. senseless
11. priceless
12. useless
13. reliable
14. undeniable
15. excitable
16. believable
17. bottomless
18. comfortable
19. dampness
20. understandable

Practice Book
Distant Voyages

© Harcourt

73

Name _____

▶ **Read each Vocabulary Word. Then write the Vocabulary Word that best completes each sentence.**

congested	**patron**	**dismantle**	**adornment**
critical	**shareholder**	**lavish**	

No one was a greater **(1)** _____ of the theater or supported it more enthusiastically than Mrs. Haley. She was an original

(2) _____ in the company that built the huge Majestic Playhouse. She was very

(3) _____ of plays that did not live up to her expectations. In fact, if a play truly displeased her, she would round up the stage crew and urge them

to **(4)** _____ the scenery before a show was over! Mrs. Haley could often be seen pushing her way through the crowds in the

(5) _____ theater lobby, wearing

an expensive, **(6)** _____ gown. A diamond wedding ring was usually her only other

(7) _____ .

SHAKESPEARE

▶ **Write the Vocabulary Word that means the opposite of each word.**

8. plain _____

9. build _____

10. complimentary _____

TRY THIS! Write a short review of a play or movie. Use at least three Vocabulary Words in your review.

Practice Book
Distant Voyages

Name _____

HOMEWORK

William
Shakespeare
& the Globe

Fact and Opinion
TEST PREP

▶ **Read the paragraph. Then circle the letter of the best answer to each question.**

Ben Jonson was a playwright of Shakespeare's time. Born in 1572, Jonson had little formal education. He first followed his stepfather's example and became a bricklayer and then became a soldier. Later he worked as an actor—a strolling player—and as a playwright. *Volpone* and *The Alchemist*, two clever and biting comedies about people obsessed with riches, are among his best works. Jonson was a generous man. About his famous competitor, Shakespeare, Jonson said, "He was not of an age, but for all time!"

1 Which statement is a fact?

A The dialogue in *Volpone* is clever and biting.

B *The Alchemist* is one of Jonson's best works.

C Shakespeare is a playwright for all time.

D Jonson worked as a strolling player.

> **Tip**
> Choose the answer that has information that can be proved to be correct or incorrect.

2 Which statement is an opinion?

F Jonson lived at the same time as Shakespeare.

G Jonson wrote clever plays.

H Jonson wrote *Volpone* and *The Alchemist*.

J Jonson had little schooling.

> **Tip**
> Which statement cannot be proved beyond a shadow of a doubt?

3 Which evidence best supports the opinion that Jonson was a generous man?

A Jonson spoke highly of his competitor.

B Jonson wrote about people who were obsessed with riches.

C Jonson followed his stepfather's example.

D Jonson was both actor and playwright.

> **Tip**
> Only one of these statements deals directly with Jonson's generosity.

© Harcourt

SCHOOL-HOME CONNECTION Help your child identify opinions in works you read together. Discuss whether the opinions are justified given the facts presented.

Practice Book
Distant Voyages

Name _____

HOMEWORK
William
Shakespeare
& the Globe
Classify/
Categorize
TEST PREP

▶ On the first line, write a category into which each group of
words fits. On the second line, add another item to that category.

1. cloud, precipitation, frost, tornado, forecast

   _____   _____

2. salmon, tuna, red snapper, herring, sardine

   _____   _____

3. collie, Labrador retriever, cocker spaniel, pug, German shepherd

   _____   _____

4. level, hammer, pliers, band saw, wrench

   _____   _____

5. smooth, rosy, short, fragrant, courageous

   _____   _____

▶ Write the word in each group that does NOT belong with the others.

6. spaghetti, lasagna, potatoes, linguine   _____

7. necessary, essential, foolish, important   _____

8. enormous, ridiculous, absurd, preposterous   _____

9. proven, reliable, trustworthy, clumsy   _____

10. kennel, bungalow, mansion, cottage   _____

© Harcourt

SCHOOL-HOME CONNECTION Challenge your
child to classify things that he or she sees every
day, such as clothing and household items, into as
many categories as possible, including size, shape, function,
and so on.

76

Practice Book
Distant Voyages

William
Shakespeare
& the Globe

Grammar:
Adjectives and
Articles

Skill Reminder • An **adjective** is a word that describes a noun or a pronoun. • **Adjectives** can tell *what kind, how many,* or *which one.* Adjectives may come before the nouns they describe. An adjective may also follow a verb such as *is, seems,* or *appears.* • The adjectives *a, an,* and *the* are called **articles.** Use *a* before a word that begins with a consonant sound. Use *an* before a word that begins with a vowel sound.

▶ Write the two adjectives in each sentence. Do not write articles. Write whether each adjective tells *what kind, how many,* or *which one.*

1. Noisy, overcrowded London really bustled during the era of Shakespeare.

   _____

2. Rich people and poor people attended the theater regularly.

   _____

3. Many playgoers saw the first production at the Globe.

   _____

4. Most playgoers were self-educated about the theater.

   _____

▶ Rewrite each sentence, completing it with the correct form of the article in parentheses ( ).

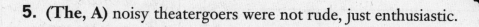

5. (The, A) noisy theatergoers were not rude, just enthusiastic.

   _____

6. (A, An) cheerful crowd ate, drank, and chatted.

   _____

7. Skillful actors could keep (the, a) attention of (a, an) audience.

   _____

8. Germania loved her first trip to (the, a) Globe.

   _____

 TRY THIS! List five things you see in the room and as many adjectives as possible to describe those items. Then write a sentence about each item, using one of the adjectives from your list.

Practice Book
Distant Voyages

Name _____

William
Shakespeare
& the Globe

Suffixes -eer, -ist,
-ian, -or, and -er

Skill Reminder • **The suffixes *-eer, -ist, -ian, -or,* and *-er* often mean "a person connected to a certain occupation" or "one who does a particular job."**

▶ Fold the paper along the dotted line. As each spelling word is read aloud, write it in the blank. Then unfold your paper, and check your work. Practice spelling any words you missed.

1. _____
2. _____
3. _____
4. _____
5. _____
6. _____
7. _____
8. _____
9. _____
10. _____
11. _____
12. _____
13. _____
14. _____
15. _____
16. _____
17. _____
18. _____
19. _____
20. _____

SPELLING WORDS

1. engineer
2. dentist
3. librarian
4. director
5. customer
6. pioneer
7. counselor
8. tourist
9. scientist
10. visitor
11. investigator
12. senator
13. astronomer
14. character
15. refrigerator
16. guardian
17. commander
18. physician
19. politician
20. leader

© Harcourt

Practice Book
Distant Voyages

Name _____

▶ **As you read the sentences, use context clues to determine the meaning of the boldfaced Vocabulary Words. Then write each Vocabulary Word next to its definition.**

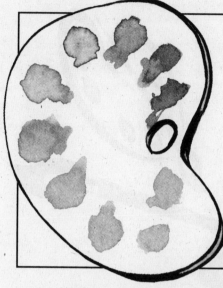

Because she loved to draw pictures, Wilma was happiest when she was **illustrating** her own stories.

During a long **series** of art lessons, Wilma's style became better and better.

Because her family praised her art, Wilma was **encouraged** to continue.

To draw the delicate colors of her favorite wildflowers, Wilma used **pastels**.

When drawing dark, stormy skies, Wilma used **charcoal**.

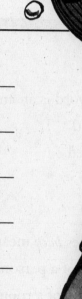

1. making pictures that go along with written material, such as books _____

2. a pencil used for drawing, made of burnt wood _____

3. a number of things that are similar to each other or related to each other _____

4. chalklike, colored sticks used for drawing _____

5. gave confidence, praise, or emotional support to another person _____

▶ **Use the Vocabulary Words to complete the newspaper article.**

Redmond Town Center is offering a **(6)** _____ of eight art classes.

The course is called "Basics of **(7)** _____." It will be given by Tim Stone, who has published four books. Students will work in black and white with

(8) _____ and in color with **(9)** _____.

Mr. Stone has **(10)** _____ many young writers and artists.

TRY THIS! Write a paragraph about something you would like to draw. Use as many Vocabulary Words as possible.

Practice Book
Distant Voyages

Name _____

HOMEWORK
The World of
William Joyce
Scrapbook

Word Relationships
TEST PREP

▶ **Read the paragraph. Circle the letter of the best answer to each question.**

When he stepped into the classroom, all eyes were on him. This was Antonio's first art class, and he was a bit nervous. He found a seat near the back and started to unpack his supplies. When the teacher entered the room and gave each student an assignment, Antonio felt more relaxed and began his first drawing. After he had worked for a while, the teacher came over and praised the picture, saying that it was very imaginative. Antonio couldn't wait to get started on his next project.

1 Which word is an antonym of *nervous*?

　A relaxed

　B worried

　C happy

　D bored

> 💡 **Tip**
> Find the sentence with *nervous*.
> Look for an antonym in the next
> few sentences.

2 What does *back* mean in this paragraph?

　F a part of a person's body

　G the rear of a room or area

　H to support or encourage

　J a football player who runs with the ball

> 💡 **Tip**
> Which meaning of *back* makes the
> most sense in this paragraph?

3 Which is a synonym of *imaginative*?

　A large

　B dark

　C dull

　D creative

> 💡 **Tip**
> Find the sentence with *imaginative*.
> Notice that it says that the teacher
> "praised" Antonio. What quality would
> the teacher most likely be praising?

© Harcourt

SCHOOL-HOME CONNECTION With your child, play a game where you say the opposite of what you mean, using antonyms.

Practice Book
Distant Voyages

Name _____

The World of
William Joyce
Scrapbook

Grammar: Proper
Adjectives

Skill Reminder • **A proper adjective** is a descriptive word formed from a proper noun. Many proper adjectives describe nationality or location. Proper adjectives are always capitalized.

▶ **Fill in the blank with the proper adjective formed from the proper noun in the parentheses ( ).**

1. I once heard a **(Spain)** _____ story about a man and a windmill.

2. Have you ever seen a **(Korea)** _____ calligraphy wall hanging?

3. My grandfather tells many **(Africa)** _____ tall tales.

4. We read a **(Russia)** _____ fairy tale together in class yesterday.

5. Our family visited the art museum to see the beautiful **(Italy)** _____ paintings.

▶ **Rewrite each sentence, replacing the words in parentheses with a proper adjective. Underline the proper adjective you wrote.**

6. Some of the most familiar children's stories were written by a **(from France)** writer.

_____

7. Other well-known stories were written by two **(from Germany)** brothers.

_____

8. Many stories are actually from **(of India)** tales. _____

_____

9. **(From Japan)** movie studios have made many monster films. _____

_____

10. Our class is reading a collection of stories by **(from South America)** authors.

_____

 TRY THIS! Skim through the travel section of the newspaper. Underline all the proper adjectives in one article. Copy five sentences that contain at least one proper adjective.

Practice Book
Distant Voyages

Name _____

Skill Reminder • The prefixes *non-* and *un-* mean "not."
• *In-* may mean "not," "in," "into," or "upon." All of these
prefixes change the meanings of base words or roots.

▶ Fold the paper along the dotted line. As each spelling word is read aloud, write it
in the blank. Then unfold your paper, and check your work. Practice spelling any
words you missed.

1. _____

2. _____

3. _____

4. _____

5. _____

6. _____

7. _____

8. _____

9. _____

10. _____

11. _____

12. _____

13. _____

14. _____

15. _____

16. _____

17. _____

18. _____

19. _____

20. _____

SPELLING WORDS

1. nontoxic
2. income
3. unknown
4. unusual
5. involved
6. unlike
7. inspector
8. unless
9. indeed
10. nonprofit
11. invisible
12. nonsense
13. incredible
14. uncomfortable
15. inconsistent
16. unfortunately
17. nonfiction
18. nonviolent
19. uncover
20. informal

© Harcourt

Practice Book
Distant Voyages

Name _____

▶ **Read the Vocabulary Words. Then write the Vocabulary Word that best completes each sentence.**

pawnshop	produce	errands	numerous	international	gravelly

1. She had many _____ to run today.

2. First, she had to go to the _____ market.

3. She wanted to get _____ odds and ends for the party.

4. Among the stores on the avenue was a _____.

5. There was also a store called "_____ Library," which sold tapes and books in many languages and from many countries.

6. She bought one tape made by a man with a deep, _____ voice.

▶ **Write the Vocabulary Word that best completes each analogy.**

7. *Bread* is to *bakery* as *vegetables* is to _____ market.

8. *Tasks* are to *responsibilities* as *trips* are to _____.

9. *One* is to *many* as *lone* is to _____.

10. *City* is to *world* as *local* is to _____.

11. *Soft* is to *gentle* as *rough* is to _____.

12. *Fruit* is to *apple* as *store* is to _____.

TRY THIS! For each Vocabulary Word, write at least three words that you associate with that word. For instance, for *produce* you might write *apples, lettuce,* and *pears.*

Practice Book
Distant Voyages

Name _____

▶ **Read the paragraph. Then circle the letter of the best answer to each question.**

Brass instruments have mouthpieces and long funnel-shaped tubes. Musicians use the mouthpieces to blow air through the tubes in order to create sounds. People make some pretty odd faces when they play brass instruments! Cornets and saxophones are excellent for jazz music. Tubas sound great in a marching band. My favorite brass instrument is the trumpet, although my brother thought playing it was very difficult.

1 Which of the following sentences is a fact about brass instruments?

A The best one is the cornet.

B Tubas sound great in a band.

C Playing the trumpet is very difficult.

D Brass instruments have long, funnel-shaped tubes.

> **Tip**
> Look for the answer choice that can be proven correct.

2 Which of the following sentences expresses the author's opinion about brass instruments?

F A tuba has a mouthpiece.

G People make odd faces playing them.

H Musicians blow air through a mouthpiece.

J Musicians can play different notes.

> **Tip**
> Look for the sentence that provides information about the author's beliefs.

3 To check the author's facts about playing brass instruments, you could

A study a diagram of an orchestra.

B read an article about classical music.

C ask a trumpet player.

D all of the above

> **Tip**
> Choose the source most likely to give you accurate information.

SCHOOL-HOME CONNECTION Help your child write a note to his or her music teacher that expresses an interest in a particular instrument. Make sure the note includes at least one sentence that is a fact and one that is an opinion.

Practice Book
Distant Voyages

© Harcourt

Skill Reminder • Adjectives can be used to compare people, places, things, or ideas. • Add *-er* to most adjectives to compare one thing with one other thing. Add *-est* to most adjectives to compare one thing with two or more other things. For adjectives of two or more syllables, use *more* instead of *-er* and *most* instead of *-est*. • Some adjectives have special forms for comparing.

▶ Underline each adjective used to compare. Then write the basic form of the adjective.

1. The trumpet has a brighter sound than the clarinet. _____

2. That banjo is bigger than a fiddle. _____

3. A piano is usually more expensive than a set of drums. _____

▶ Rewrite each sentence, using the correct form of the adjective in parentheses ( ).

4. Santiago's horn was (**small**) than the one in the pawnshop. _____

   _____

5. Louis made up his mind that he would play the (**hot**) horn in New Orleans. _____

   _____

6. When Bunk Johnson waved to him, Louis was the (**proud**) stepper in the whole

   parade. _____

   _____

▶ In the blank following the sentence, write the correct form of the adjective in parentheses ( ).

7. When Louis blew the second time, the noise was even (**bad**). _____

8. For Louis, the horn was a (**good**) instrument than the banjo. _____

Skill Reminder • **The prefix *re-* means "back" or "again."**
***Inter-* usually means "between." Both prefixes will change the meanings of
base words or roots.**

▶ **Fold the paper along the dotted line. As each spelling word is read aloud, write it
in the blank. Then unfold your paper, and check your work. Practice spelling any
words you missed.**

1. _____
2. _____
3. _____
4. _____
5. _____
6. _____
7. _____
8. _____
9. _____
10. _____
11. _____
12. _____
13. _____
14. _____
15. _____
16. _____
17. _____
18. _____
19. _____
20. _____

SPELLING WORDS

1. remove
2. interview
3. repeat
4. interrupt
5. respect
6. interfere
7. represent
8. relocate
9. international
10. review
11. interpret
12. interstate
13. remarkable
14. intermediate
15. intersection
16. recommend
17. interject
18. intervene
19. resource
20. remained

© Harcourt

Name _____

▶ **Read the Vocabulary Words. Then read the groups of words below. Write the Vocabulary Word that is most closely related to each group of words.**

| migrant | timid | flexibility | devote | scholarship | thrived | apprentice |

quiet	frightened	fearful	1. _____
traveling	workers	agriculture	2. _____
grew	succeeded	flourished	3. _____
beginner	skill	trainee	4. _____
bendable	yielding	adaptable	5. _____
dedicate	time	goal	6. _____
education	money	tuition	7. _____

▶ **Write the Vocabulary Word that best completes each sentence.**

8. The head of the ballet troupe began her career as an _____.

9. She had to _____ most of her time to perfecting her skills.

10. Her natural grace and _____ made it easy for her to perform the most difficult dances.

11. She was _____ when she began her training, but she gradually became more confident.

12. She _____ because so many people encouraged her.

Name _____

HOMEWORK
Evelyn Cisneros:
Prima Ballerina
**Main Idea
and Details**
TEST PREP

▶ **Read the paragraph. Then circle the letter of the best answer to each question.**

A ballet class is a training session that consists of three parts. The first part is a series of warm-up exercises, performed at a waist-high railing called a *barre*. The second part of the session consists of slow work. The dancer practices holding a position and maintaining balance. The final part of the session consists of fast work. This is when the dancer does the big leaps and turns across the floor that make ballet such a dazzling sight.

1 What is the main idea of the paragraph?

  A A ballet class has warm-up exercises.

  B A ballet class includes slow work.

  C A ballet class is a three-part training session.

  D A ballet class includes fast work.

> 💡 **Tip**
> Look for the sentence that summarizes the paragraph.

2 Which is NOT a detail in the paragraph?

  F The waist-high practice railing is called the *barre*.

  G A ballet class lasts two hours.

  H A dancer does slow work in the second part of a ballet class.

  J Big jumps and turns are practiced in the third part of the class.

> 💡 **Tip**
> Reread the paragraph to see which detail it does not include.

3 Which of these additional details would fit into this paragraph?

  A Ballet dancers wear dazzling costumes when they perform.

  B Classical ballet is sometimes called Romantic ballet.

  C Most ballet performances have three parts.

  D The final part of a ballet class is called *allegro*, which means "fast work."

> 💡 **Tip**
> Remember that the main idea of the paragraph has to do with a ballet *class*.

SCHOOL-HOME CONNECTION Help your child to write a main idea sentence stating whether he or she likes ballet. Then make a list of details that support the main idea.

88

Practice Book
Distant Voyages

© Harcourt

Skill Reminder • A **verb** expresses action or being. When a verb includes two or more words, it is called a **verb phrase**. The **main verb** is the most important word in a verb phrase. A **helping verb** can work with the main verb to tell about an action.

▶ Underline the verb phrase in each sentence. Write the main verb.

1. The San Francisco Ballet had finished its performance. _____

2. In *The Sleeping Beauty*, the princess had found her prince. _____

3. On its feet, the audience was clapping wildly. _____

4. We could hear shouts of "Brava!" _____

▶ Underline each helping verb once and each main verb twice.

5. The Cisneros family had moved to Huntington Beach.

6. The neighborhood children were teasing Evelyn.

7. Because of her shyness, she would not talk in school.

8. By the end of the year, Evelyn was taking ballet lessons.

▶ Rewrite each sentence, adding the word in parentheses to the verb phrase.

9. Evelyn did mind hard work. **(not)**

_____

_____

10. She had done well in junior high school sports. **(always)**

_____

_____

© Harcourt

Practice Book
Distant Voyages

Skill Reminder • The syllable *dis-* at the beginning of a word may be a prefix that means "not" or "the opposite of."

• The syllable *de-* at the beginning of a word may be a prefix that means "from," "down," "off," "away," "of," or "out."

▶ Fold the paper along the dotted line. As each spelling word is read aloud, write it in the blank. Then unfold your paper, and check your work. Practice spelling any words you missed.

1. _____
2. _____
3. _____
4. _____
5. _____
6. _____
7. _____
8. _____
9. _____
10. _____
11. _____
12. _____
13. _____
14. _____
15. _____
16. _____
17. _____
18. _____
19. _____
20. _____

SPELLING WORDS

1. discuss
2. deduct
3. dismissed
4. develop
5. disease
6. discount
7. disturb
8. details
9. demand
10. determined
11. depressed
12. defense
13. disappointing
14. discouraged
15. disadvantage
16. demonstrated
17. defeat
18. descent
19. disappear
20. disconnect

© Harcourt

Practice Book
Distant Voyages

▶ **Read the Vocabulary Words. Then write the Vocabulary Word that best completes each sentence.**

campaign   residence   obnoxious   endorse   graffiti

1. The woman's _____ was in an apartment building.

2. Someone painted _____ on the building's white wall.

3. She reported this _____ behavior to the mayor's office.

4. One of the mayor's _____ promises had been to keep the city clean.

5. The mayor decided to _____ a plan to begin block cleanup patrols.

▶ **Write the Vocabulary Word that goes with each group of words.**

6. unpleasant   irritating   rude   _____

7. tactics   crusade   headquarters   _____

8. promote   confirm   encourage   _____

9. home   dwelling   apartment   _____

10. paint   words   walls   _____

▶ **Complete these analogies using the Vocabulary Words.**

11. car : garage : : person : _____

12. worker : job : : candidate : _____

13. no : reject : : yes : _____

14. polite : rude : : nice : _____

15. litter : park : : _____ : building

TRY THIS! Write two sentences that contain two or more of the Vocabulary Words.

Practice Book
Distant Voyages

Name _____

▶ **Read the paragraph. Then circle the letter of the best answer to each question.**

Mayoral candidates Sue Clark and Alberto Muñoz are both trying to appeal to voters. Both have run TV ads and spoken publicly. Ms. Clark's first priority is to improve city schools. Mr. Muñoz also says he is for school improvement. Though the candidates agree on that issue, the similarities end there. Clark wants smaller class size, but Muñoz thinks the answer is more testing. On the parking issue, Clark wants meters in the shopping district. In contrast, Muñoz supports a free parking garage. The voters will decide on Tuesday.

1 On what issue do the candidates agree?

  A election reform

  B improving the schools

  C new parking meters

  D a free parking garage

> **Tip**
> Look for words like *both*, *also*, *too*, *similarly*, and *alike* to find issues the candidates agree on.

2 Which issue is NOT part of Ms. Clark's platform?

  F improving the schools

  G smaller class size

  H new parking meters

  J more testing

> **Tip**
> Notice the key word NOT in the question.

3 In what other way are the candidates alike?

  A They are trying to get their message to the voters.

  B They have already begun work on school improvement.

  C They have a plan for election reform.

  D They belong to the same political party.

> **Tip**
> Read the answer choices carefully. Some cannot be supported by the passage.

SCHOOL-HOME CONNECTION Imagine you and your child are opponents in an election for mayor in your community. Compare and contrast the issues in each of your election platforms.

92

© Harcourt

Name _____

▶ **Read the story, and fill in the chart. Determine the character traits of each girl, and list them in the first column. Then list supporting details from the story in the second column.**

| observant | impatient | fidgety | imaginative | nature-loving | outspoken |

Janelle and Ivy were drifting in a rowboat in the middle of Duck Lake. Their baited poles were hanging over the edge of the boat. Janelle was watching the dragonflies and thinking how graceful they were. Ivy interrupted her observations.

"Can't we go back yet? It is so boring out here! Besides, these must be smart fish—they are staying far away from us!"

"Ivy," said Janelle, "relax and enjoy the view. Look at the reflections of the clouds on the water. The lake is like a mirror today!" Janelle pointed out a cloud that looked like a giant and another that looked like an airplane.

Ivy was not impressed. As she nervously tapped her foot on the bottom of the boat and twirled her hair around her finger, she said, "Why don't we go back and go swimming or ride our bikes? I hate just sitting!"

Suddenly the line on Ivy's fishing pole got tight. Ivy slowly reeled in a fish. As it flopped into the boat, Ivy screamed, "What do I do now?"

Janelle calmly took Ivy's line, unhooked the fish, and gently put it back in the lake.

"What did you do that for? I just waited an hour to get that fish!" exclaimed Ivy.

"You didn't really think we were going to keep the fish, did you?" asked Janelle. "I catch and release the fish. I fish for the sport of it."

"Well, I think it's a pretty dumb sport. Let's get out of here," said Ivy.

	Character Traits	Evidence from the Story
Janelle	1.	
	2.	
	3.	
Ivy	1.	
	2.	
	3.	

SCHOOL-HOME CONNECTION Read a story with your child. Discuss one of the characters. What character traits does he or she have?

93

Practice Book
Distant Voyages

© Harcourt

Skill Reminder • An **action verb** tells what the subject of a sentence does, did, or will do. An action verb is often followed by a **direct object,** a noun or pronoun that receives the action. • **A linking verb** connects the subject to a noun, pronoun, or adjective in the predicate that renames or describes the subject. The most common linking verbs are forms of *be: am, is, are, was, were.*

▶ Fill in the blanks with verbs. The words in parentheses ( ) at the end of each sentence indicate the kind of verb you should choose.

1. Joey _____ into the kitchen. **(action verb)**

2. His eyes _____ thick with sleep. **(linking verb)**

3. The family _____ a large breakfast. **(action verb)**

4. The food _____ especially good. **(linking verb)**

▶ Copy each sentence, and underline the verb once. Circle any noun or adjective that follows a linking verb. Draw two lines under any direct object. Then write whether each verb is *action* or *linking*.

5. After breakfast Miata and Papi washed the dishes. _____

_____

6. The soapy water felt very hot. _____

_____

7. Miata's mother made an appointment with Doña Carmen. _____

_____

8. Doña Carmen had been a mayor. _____

_____

TRY THIS! *Feel, grow, look,* and *taste* can all be both linking and action verbs. Example: I feel hot. (linking); I feel the prickly leaves. (action). Write sentences using *grow, look,* and *taste* as both linking and action verbs.

Practice Book
Distant Voyages

Skill Reminder • The prefix *pre-* usually means "before."
• The prefix *pro-* means "for" or "on behalf of."
• Both prefixes change the meaning of the root.

▶ Fold the paper along the dotted line. As each spelling word is read aloud, write it in the blank. Then unfold your paper, and check your work. Practice spelling any words you missed.

1. _____
2. _____
3. _____
4. _____
5. _____
6. _____
7. _____
8. _____
9. _____
10. _____
11. _____
12. _____
13. _____
14. _____
15. _____
16. _____
17. _____
18. _____
19. _____
20. _____

SPELLING WORDS

1. prevent
2. program
3. predict
4. project
5. pretend
6. process
7. prefer
8. promise
9. previous
10. protect
11. property
12. propose
13. precede
14. proceed
15. pronunciation
16. professional
17. pretest
18. preview
19. proclaim
20. progress

Practice Book
Distant Voyages

▶ **Write the Vocabulary Word that best completes each analogy.**

| polio | astonished | dismay |
| decipher | immobility | despised |

1. *Calm* is to *peaceful* as *amazed* is to _____.

2. *Medicine* is to *penicillin* as *disease* is to _____.

3. *Laughter* is to *tears* as *movement* is to _____.

4. *Loved* is to *cared* as *scorned* is to _____.

5. *Smile* is to *joy* as *frown* is to _____.

6. *Study* is to *learn* as *analyze* is to _____.

▶ **Write the correct Vocabulary Word to complete each sentence.**

7. _____ had left Ted unable to move his legs.

8. He _____ the thought of giving in to his illness.

9. Though he felt great _____, he was determined to succeed.

10. Although his physical _____ prevented him from walking, his brain functioned extremely well.

11. He learned to _____ even the most difficult codes.

12. His great ability soon _____ experts.

TRY THIS! Write a paragraph about a spy who uses a secret code to communicate. Use at least three Vocabulary Words in your paragraph.

Practice Book
Distant Voyages

© Harcourt

▶ **Read the paragraph. Then circle the letter of the best answer to each question.**

Mainstreaming means that all students, even those with disabilities, are taught in the same classroom. Having students in class like Peter, who is in a wheelchair, and Ellin, who is blind, seems very natural. Peter and Ellin do the same things as the rest of us, but they do things a little differently. After all, each of us can do some things better than others. Mainstreaming is an idea that works for all students.

1 Which statement expresses the author's viewpoint about mainstreaming?

  A It should not be used in classrooms.

  B It is a bad idea.

  C It is something that works for all students.

  D It works for some students.

> **Tip**
> Reread the paragraph to find at least one sentence that expresses the author's opinion about mainstreaming.

2 What evidence supports the author's opinion?

  F Two students with disabilities fit into the classroom well.

  G The author's parents support mainstreaming.

  H The author knows two students with disabilities who are very smart.

  J Two students with disabilities have become the author's best friends.

> **Tip**
> What has been the impact of having students with disabilities in the author's classroom?

3 Which is probably NOT a reason why the author wrote the paragraph?

  A to express personal feelings

  B to give an opinion

  C to entertain

  D to give information about mainstreaming

> **Tip**
> Judging from the subject and how the author wrote about it, which reason was not very important?

© Harcourt

SCHOOL-HOME CONNECTION With your child, read an editorial in a newspaper. Discuss the editor's purpose and perspective. What evidence does the editor use to support his or her opinion?

97

Practice Book
Distant Voyages

Skill Reminder • The **tense of a verb** tells the time of an action. There are three basic verb tenses: **present, past,** and **future**. A present-tense verb shows that the action is happening now or happens over and over. • The form of a present-tense verb changes to agree with the subject of the sentence. This is called **subject-verb agreement**.

▶ **Circle the present-tense verbs in these sentences.**

1. Jean turns sideways at her new desk.

2. Over her shoulder, she glimpses Shirley Russell.

3. Shirley's golden ringlets curl and shine like Shirley Temple's.

4. All the students in Jean's class like Shirley and want to be her best friend.

▶ **Rewrite each sentence. Choose the verb form in parentheses ( ) that agrees with the subject of the sentence.**

5. Miss Marr **(type, types)** Jean's words for her on a large-print typewriter.

_____

_____

6. During recess, the students **(make, makes)** a lot of noise.

_____

_____

7. Jean **(believe, believes)** that Miss Marr has asked Shirley to do something impossible.

_____

_____

8. She **(stare, stares)** off into the distance and **(think, thinks)** about how she will complete the assignment.

_____

_____

TRY THIS! Choose a person in your classroom to observe. Write a paragraph in the present tense about what she or he does.

© Harcourt

Name _____

Skill Reminder • In most words with the VCCV pattern, the syllable break occurs between the two consonants in the middle of the word.
• In VCCV words, the accent may be on either the first or the second syllable.

▶ Fold the paper along the dotted line. As each spelling word is read aloud, write it in the blank. Then unfold your paper, and check your work. Practice spelling any words you missed.

1. _____
2. _____
3. _____
4. _____
5. _____
6. _____
7. _____
8. _____
9. _____
10. _____
11. _____
12. _____
13. _____
14. _____
15. _____
16. _____
17. _____
18. _____
19. _____
20. _____

SPELLING WORDS

1. pretty
2. service
3. thunder
4. blanket
5. effort
6. fellow
7. subject
8. perhaps
9. attack
10. entire
11. chimney
12. tunnel
13. effect
14. suspended
15. challenge
16. pretzel
17. survive
18. pillow
19. hunger
20. college

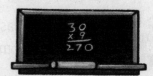

Practice Book
Distant Voyages

© Harcourt

Name _____

▶ **Read the Vocabulary Words. Then write the Vocabulary Word that best completes each sentence.**

insulated	muffle	partition	prowls
refinery	grade	submitted	

1. At night, a raccoon _____ around the trash bins, looking for food.

2. The bins are outside the cafeteria of the sugar _____.

3. A thick wall has been built to _____ the machinery noises for nearby residents.

4. Workers have _____ this wall to keep the heat in.

5. Loaded trucks drive up a steep _____ near the plant.

6. Today the company president _____ his yearly status report.

7. A _____ was set up in the cafeteria before the president began his speech.

▶ **Write the Vocabulary Word that completes each web.**

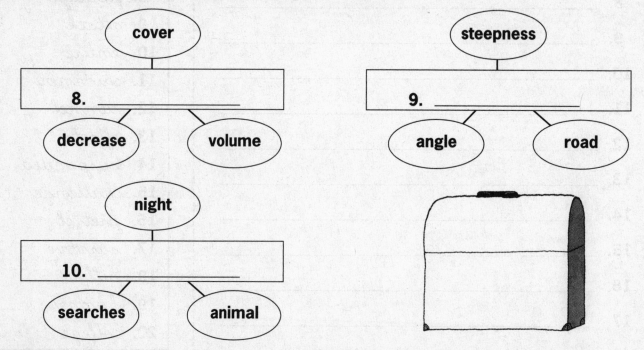

cover

8. _____

decrease   volume

steepness

9. _____

angle   road

night

10. _____

searches   animal

TRY THIS! Look in the classified section of the newspaper to find out what job opportunities exist in the community. Cut out advertisements that use any of the Vocabulary Words.

© Harcourt

Name _____

▶ **Read the paragraph. Circle the letter of the best answer to each question.**

Lee had never thought of what kind of job he wanted until his teacher asked him. Maybe he could be a writer? It was fun making up stories about people and places. However, he wondered what he would do if he couldn't sell any books. How would he earn money? He also considered being a truck driver like his father. He knew that truck drivers see different parts of the country rather than just write about them. He also knew that they don't worry about selling enough books to earn a paycheck. Yet Lee knew that driving could be dangerous—especially in bad weather. Lee was glad he didn't have to make a decision for a while!

1 The writer compares the two jobs by focusing on

　A the advantages of being a writer.

　B the disadvantages of being a writer.

　C the disadvantages of being a truck driver.

　D the advantages and disadvantages of each job.

> **Tip**
> Review the things the writer says about each job, and choose the answer that best reflects what you've read.

2 After making the comparison, the writer concludes that

　F truck driving is better.

　G writing is better.

　H Lee should think of a third kind of job.

　J Lee is lucky he doesn't have to decide right away.

> **Tip**
> Remember that a conclusion often comes at the end of a paragraph.

3 Someone who chose to become a writer instead of a truck driver might

　A want a regular paycheck.

　B enjoy studying people's characters.

　C enjoy working outdoors.

　D like to drive in bad weather.

> **Tip**
> Think about which answer choice describes something that would appeal to a writer.

SCHOOL-HOME CONNECTION Discuss with your child two jobs that interest him or her. Together, think of two ways in which the jobs are similar. Then think of two ways in which the jobs are different.

Practice Book
Distant Voyages

© Harcourt

Skill Reminder • A verb in the **past tense** shows that the action happened in the past. Form the past tense of most verbs by adding *-ed*.
• A verb in the **future tense** shows that the action will happen in the future. Form the future tense of a verb by using the helping verb *will*.

▶ Underline the verb in each sentence once. Then identify the tense of the verb as *past* or *future*.

1. The girls loved Mrs. Badger's books. _____

2. All the students will help themselves at the salad bar. _____

3. The boys and girls carried their plates back to the table. _____

4. Lee tried some interesting food. _____

▶ Rewrite these sentences, using the tense of the verb in parentheses ( ) that makes the most sense.

5. Lee **(attend)** the special lunch tomorrow. _____
_____

6. "I **(read)** your story last week, Lee," Mrs. Badger said. _____
_____

7. At yesterday's lunch, Mrs. Badger **(call)** Lee an author. _____
_____

8. "I thought that you **(describe)** the truck ride very well," she said. _____
_____

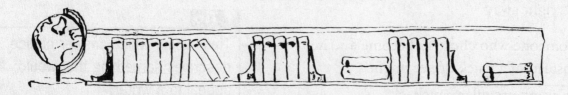

TRY THIS! Reread a paper you have written for a previous assignment. Check your writing for verbs in the past and future tenses. See if you can find three verbs in the past tense and three verbs in the future tense. Write a list of the verbs you find.

© Harcourt

Skill Reminder • Just add *-ed* or *-ing* to words with an unstressed final syllable. • Double the final consonant before adding *-ed* or *-ing* to words of one syllable or a stressed final syllable that ends in a single vowel and consonant (*stop*).

▶ Fold the paper along the dotted line. As each spelling word is read aloud, write it in the blank. Then unfold your paper, and check your work. Practice spelling any words you missed.

1. _____
2. _____
3. _____
4. _____
5. _____
6. _____
7. _____
8. _____
9. _____
10. _____
11. _____
12. _____
13. _____
14. _____
15. _____
16. _____
17. _____
18. _____
19. _____
20. _____

SPELLING WORDS

1. wondering
2. fastened
3. permitting
4. controlled
5. listening
6. regretted
7. suffered
8. admitted
9. referred
10. bothered
11. submitted
12. whispered
13. transferred
14. occurring
15. canceled
16. developing
17. scrubbing
18. upsetting
19. wondered
20. quarreled

© Harcourt

Name _____

▶ **As you read the paragraph, use context clues to determine the meaning of the boldfaced Vocabulary Words. Then write each Vocabulary Word next to its correct definition.**

I had a dream last night. In it, I inherited $10 million and went on a fabulous shopping spree. There was no limit to what I could buy! First, I took my private limousine to the downtown shopping mall. I searched every **aisle** of every store until I found the perfect stereo. There were many other fun gadgets that caught my eye, but I didn't let them **sidetrack** me.

Next, I boarded my private jet and was whisked away to Paris. Every salesperson was **beaming** and eager to assist me. I guess I already had the **reputation** of a millionaire. As I began to spend my money, I realized that I couldn't stop myself. I was so **absorbed** in spending it, I suddenly found myself penniless and miserable.

When I woke up with a start, I took an **oath** to be content with what I had.

1. a walkway _____

2. fame, character, good name _____

3. smiling broadly _____

4. to turn aside, distract _____

5. a solemn promise _____

6. totally interested _____

▶ **Write the Vocabulary Word that best completes each analogy.**

7. *Push* is to *pull* as *frowning* is to _____.

8. *Street* is to *sidewalk* as *auditorium* is to _____.

9. *Funny* is to *joke* as *serious* is to _____.

10. *Fact* is to *truth* as *character* is to _____.

11. *Draw* is to *attract* as *distract* is to _____.

TRY THIS!
Suppose you inherited $10 million. Using at least three Vocabulary Words, write a paragraph describing what you would do with the money.

© Harcourt

Name _____

HOMEWORK
Frindle

Author's
Perspective/
Author's Purpose
TEST PREP

▶ **Read the paragraph. Then circle the letter of the best answer to each question.**

    In my years as a forest ranger, I've watched many forests become thinner and thinner. Every year more and more of the earth's resources are being used up. Humans cut down rain forests, consume fossil fuels, and also pollute the land and air. If we continue to destroy the earth recklessly, there will be nothing left for future generations. We must act responsibly and take care of the earth, not only for ourselves, but also for the other animals on this planet.

1 What is the author's purpose in this passage?

  A to encourage more visitors to visit national forests

  B to persuade people to take better care of the planet

  C to threaten campers who carelessly set fires

  D to entertain with stories of the great outdoors

 Tip
Think of the kinds of details the author presents. What do these details suggest about the author's purpose?

2 What perspective does the author bring to this topic?

  F The author is a forest ranger who has witnessed destruction of natural resources.

  G The author is a forest ranger who wants loggers to keep their jobs.

  H The author is a person who loves to camp in the wilderness.

  J The author has written several survival guides.

Tip
Think about the author's work, as well as the author's experiences with and feelings about the outdoors.

3 Which of these statements would the author probably NOT agree with?

  A People need to keep the earth beautiful for future generations.

  B People should leave the earth in a suitable state for animals.

  C People should not use public lands.

  D People should use public lands carefully.

Tip
To answer this question, consider what you have and have not learned about the author's views from this passage.

SCHOOL-HOME CONNECTION With your child, search through a newspaper for a persuasive article. Then ask him or her to explain the author's perspective.

Practice Book
Distant Voyages

Skill Reminder • The principal parts of a verb are the infinitive, the present participle, the past, and the past participle. Participles in verb phrases are forms used with helping verbs.

▶ Label the underlined verb form in each sentence as *present participle*, *past*, or *past participle*.

1. Mrs. Granger was <u>beaming</u> at Nick as he sat in his chair.

_____

2. He <u>raised</u> his hand without waiting for Mrs. Granger to call on him.

_____

3. Nick, completely absorbed in his thoughts, <u>bumped</u> into Jane.

_____

4. Nick was <u>standing</u> in front of the counter at the store.

_____

5. When asked for a frindle, the clerk <u>reached</u> for a pen.

_____

6. The plan had <u>worked</u>—the pen was now a frindle.

_____

▶ Rewrite the sentences, using a form of the verb in parentheses ( ) and the participle that fits best.

7. Nick has **(transform)** _____ his classroom. _____

_____

8. Nick and Janet are **(miss)** _____ the bus because of the meeting. _____

_____

9. The teacher was **(point)** _____ at the dictionary. _____

_____

10. All the students had **(raise)** _____ their hands to make the oath. _____

_____

Name _____

Skill Reminder • **To spell a two-syllable word that has three consonants in the middle, divide the word into syllables. If two consonants form a blend, divide the word before or after those two consonants. Then spell the word one syllable at a time.**

▶ Fold the paper along the dotted line. As each spelling word is read aloud, write it in the blank. Then unfold your paper, and check your work. Practice spelling any words you missed.

1. _____
2. _____
3. _____
4. _____
5. _____
6. _____
7. _____
8. _____
9. _____
10. _____
11. _____
12. _____
13. _____
14. _____
15. _____
16. _____
17. _____
18. _____
19. _____
20. _____

SPELLING WORDS

1. subtract
2. distract
3. contract
4. complex
5. distrust
6. extra
7. improve
8. instead
9. Congress
10. English
11. conflict
12. exchange
13. pumpkin
14. sandwich
15. Christmas
16. construction
17. luncheon
18. complaint
19. transform
20. although

Practice Book
Distant Voyages

Name _____

▶ **Write the Vocabulary Word that best completes each sentence.**

sorrowfully	loftily	dispute
adjusted	nonchalantly	

Smiling **(1)** _____, Tasha looked up sadly from the computer game she was playing with her best friend, Mollie. "I'm sorry I can't finish the game," she said slowly. "I'm running out of energy."

"How can you be out of energy already?" Molly said. "We just started this game! Now that we've got all the controls **(2)** _____ just right, you want to quit! Besides, I *never* run out of energy," she added,

tossing her head **(3)** _____.

"I won't **(4)** _____ that statement, but I'm different," Tasha said. "I can take care of the problem, though."

Calmly, Tasha stood up and walked into the next room. There, she

(5) _____ opened the compartment in her side and inserted fresh robot batteries.

▶ **Write the Vocabulary Word that fits in each word group.**

6. calmly, casually, _____

7. quarrel, disagree, _____

8. sadly, mournfully, _____

9. fixed, set, _____

10. proudly, arrogantly, _____

TRY THIS! The Vocabulary Words *nonchalantly*, *sorrowfully*, and *loftily* are adverbs, words that tell more about verbs. Reread a page in the story, and list all the adverbs you find. Then explain what additional information they give about the verbs.

© Harcourt

Name _____

▶ **Read the paragraph. Then circle the letter of the best answer to each question.**

Though only a few are left, one-room schoolhouses hold a special place in Americans' imaginations. At their best, these tiny schools hummed with activity as students of various ages worked at the levels that suited them. Older students helped teach younger students, and the teacher maintained discipline. Of course, one-room schoolhouses were not perfect. Teachers' training varied greatly and some had no special training. Sometimes older students slept through class.

1 Which conclusion about one-room schoolhouses is most reasonable?

A One-room schoolhouses are perfect places to learn.

B One-room schoolhouses damage students.

C One-room schoolhouses have many good features.

D We should build more one-room schoolhouses.

💡 **Tip**
Which conclusion reflects both positive and negative things about one-room schoolhouses?

2 Which fact or detail best supports the conclusion above?

F Students worked at the levels that suited them.

G Some students slept through class.

H Teachers did not always have special training.

J Only a few one-room schoolhouses remain today.

💡 **Tip**
The answer to question 2 should follow logically from question 1.

3 Which conclusion is NOT justified by the information in the paragraph?

A Americans have sentimental feelings about one-room schoolhouses.

B Teachers at one-room schools had to deal with many different types of students.

C Everyone who attended a one-room schoolhouse graduated.

D One-room schoolhouses are mostly a thing of the past.

💡 **Tip**
Eliminate choices that are clearly stated in the paragraph.

SCHOOL-HOME CONNECTION Analyze a television show with your child. What conclusions, based on evidence, can he or she draw about the characters?

Practice Book
Distant Voyages

© Harcourt

Name _____

Skill Reminder • **Regular verbs** are verbs that end in *-ed* in
the past tense. • **Irregular verbs** are verbs that do not end in
-ed in the past tense. Irregular verbs have special spellings for the
past and past participle.

▶ **Choose the correct verb form of the two in parentheses ( ), and write it on the line.**

1. Ari **(go, went)** quickly toward his personal transport vehicle. _____

2. Dean **(run, ran)** by his side. _____

3. Ari **(speaked, spoke)** excitedly to his friend. _____

4. "I had **(mean, meant)** to bring the rapid release module

   with me," he told Dean. _____

5. "I **(forget, forgot)** because I was hurrying so fast." _____

▶ **Rewrite each sentence, using the correct past or past participle of the verb in
parentheses ( ).**

6. The personal transport vehicle had **(come)** into plain view in front of the boys.

   _____

   _____

7. "I remembered to bring the module along," Dean **(say)** to Ari.

   _____

   _____

8. He pulled out the rapid release module and **(begin)** to set the code.

   _____

   _____

**TRY
THIS!** Make a list of verbs that you could use to tell how space vehicles move and
function. Draw an asterisk by the irregular verbs.

Name _____

Skill Reminder • **If a vowel sound in the first syllable is long, the syllable break comes before the consonant (V/CV).** • **If the vowel sound in the first syllable is short, the break comes after the consonant (VC/V).**

▶ Fold the paper along the dotted line. As each spelling word is read aloud, write it in the blank. Then unfold your paper, and check your work. Practice spelling any words you missed.

1. _____

2. _____

3. _____

4. _____

5. _____

6. _____

7. _____

8. _____

9. _____

10. _____

11. _____

12. _____

13. _____

14. _____

15. _____

16. _____

17. _____

18. _____

19. _____

20. _____

SPELLING WORDS

1. slogan
2. radar
3. minutes
4. honest
5. second
6. virus
7. shadow
8. humor
9. salad
10. eleven
11. closet
12. model
13. volcano
14. private
15. balance
16. radio
17. basis
18. decent
19. fanatic
20. novel

© Harcourt

111

Practice Book
Distant Voyages

▶ Write the Vocabulary Word that best completes each sentence in the conversation.

rigging	furl	huddled	vast
beams	lurked	settlement	

1. What were you doing climbing up in the _____?

2. Well, I had to _____ one of the sails and tie it to the mast.

3. Do you think it will be a long time after our ship lands before we can establish a _____?

4. No. Even though the ocean is _____, we can cross it fairly quickly.

5. I heard the groaning of the _____ as we sailed last night in the storm.

6. I heard the whimpering of a dog who _____ in the corner. Was that your dog?

7. Yes! We were all _____ together for warmth last night, but we couldn't comfort our dog.

▶ Use Vocabulary Words to complete the sentence below.

The people crossed the **(8)** _____ ocean, hoping to establish

a **(9)** _____ in Virginia, where they could use strong

(10) _____ of wood to build homes.

TRY THIS! Write a dialogue between two people on a ship. Try to use all the Vocabulary Words in your dialogue.

© Harcourt

Practice Book
Distant Voyages

Name _____

▶ **Read the paragraph. Then circle the letter of the best answer to each question.**

The ship's passengers stood on deck. They watched the approaching dark clouds. Then the storm broke. The wind howled and the rain pounded, chasing everyone to the lower deck. The tiny ship shuddered as it rose and fell in the rough sea. Waves as high as mountains swept over the deck. Some people cried, and a young boy huddled with his father in a protected corner. "Don't go away from me, Papa!" he cried in terror.

1 Which idea about the wind does the word *howled* express?

  A The wind moaned softly.

  B The wind blew gently like a breeze.

  C The wind blew noisily and steadily.

  D The wind was like a person singing.

> **Tip**
> Ask yourself, "If something howls, what does it do?"

2 What meaning does the word *shuddered* suggest?

  F swung or swayed

  G shook, as if in fear

  H pounded

  J moved silently

> **Tip**
> Think about what you would be doing if you shuddered.

3 Which statement conveys the strong negative connotation of the last sentence?

  A "Don't leave me, Papa!"

  B "Don't depart, Papa!"

  C "Don't retreat, Papa!"

  D "Don't abandon me, Papa!"

> **Tip**
> Which verb tells the worst thing that could happen to the young boy?

© Harcourt

SCHOOL-HOME CONNECTION Help your child rewrite the paragraph on this page. Replace *howled* and *shuddered,* and two more words that you choose, with synonyms. Do the new words change the picture the author is trying to convey? Write a short explanation.

113

Name _____

▶ **Look at the reference books shown below. Then read the information for each item below. Write the name of the best reference source to answer the question.**

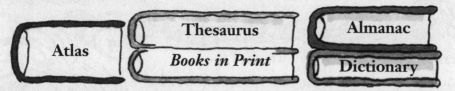

Atlas   Thesaurus   Almanac

Books in Print   Dictionary

1. Steve read the selection "Across the Wide Dark Sea." Now he wants to know exactly where Plymouth, Massachusetts is located. Where is the best place to look for this

information? _____

2. When Steve read the selection, he came across the word *mussels*. Where should he

look to find the meaning of this word? _____

3. Steve also came across the word *journey* in the story. He wondered if there were other words with similar meanings. Where should Steve look for this information?

_____

4. Steve wants to find the title of another book by Jean Van Leeuwen, the author of "Across the Wide Dark Sea." Where could he find a listing of this author's current

books? _____

5. Where could Steve find a census report for the current population of Massachusetts?

_____

6. Steve would like to trace the route taken by the *Mayflower*. The ship traveled across the Atlantic Ocean from Plymouth, England, to Plymouth, Massachusetts. Where can Steve

see this information? _____

7. Steve found the following information:

an·chor (ang′kər), *n.*
   1. A heavy piece of iron or steel lowered into
the water to hold a ship in place.
   2. Something that makes a person feel secure.

From what reference source did this information come?

_____

Name _____

▶ Answer the questions about using an encyclopedia.

| A | B | C–Ch | Ci–Cz | D | E | F | G | H | I | J–K | L | M | N–O | P | Q–R | S–Sn | So–Sz | T | U–V | W–X | Y–Z |

1. After visiting Plymouth Plantation in Massachusetts, Sylvia wanted to learn more about the Pilgrims. Which volume of the encyclopedia would she use to find

   information about them? _____

2. Which volume might have information

   about the state where the Pilgrims landed? _____

▶ Use this table of contents from a book about the Pilgrims to help you answer questions 3–5.

3. Where would you look for the meaning of the word *Puritans*? _____

4. Where would you find suggestions for further reading about the Pilgrims?

   _____

5. Where would you find the author's exact source for the cost of building a ship like

   the *Mayflower*? _____

▶ Write three key words you would use to search the Internet for information about the Pilgrims.

6. _____   7. _____   8. _____

SCHOOL-HOME CONNECTION Name several topics. Ask your child to tell you the encyclopedia volume that would most likely have information on each topic.

Practice Book
Distant Voyages

© Harcourt

Name _____

Skill Reminder • A verb in the **present perfect tense** shows that the action started to happen sometime before now. • A verb in the **past perfect tense** shows that the action happened before a specific time in the past. • A verb in the **future perfect tense** shows that the action will have happened before a specific time in the future.

▶ In each sentence, underline the verb phrase and circle the main verb. Then write whether the verb is in the *present perfect, past perfect,* or *future perfect* tense.

1. By sunrise everyone had crowded on deck. _____

2. A low, dark outline between sea and land has appeared. _____

3. My mother had never smiled so much. _____

4. By noon, the ship will have reached land. _____

▶ Rewrite each sentence with the verb and tense shown in parentheses ( ).

5. A party of men in a small boat _____ off to explore. (**go**, **present perfect**)

_____

_____

6. Before evening, they _____ armfuls of firewood. (**gather**, **past perfect**)

_____

_____

7. They told tales of what they _____ in the new land. (**see**, **past perfect**)

_____

_____

8. "By winter," said my father, "I hope we _____ the right place for our settlement." (**find**, **future perfect**)

_____

_____

© Harcourt

Practice Book
Distant Voyages

Name _____

Skill Reminder When a word has two different vowel sounds between two consonants, divide the word between the two vowel sounds. Then spell the word one syllable at a time.

▶ Fold the paper along the dotted line. As each spelling word is read aloud, write it in the blank. Then unfold your paper, and check your work. Practice spelling any words you missed.

1. _____
2. _____
3. _____
4. _____
5. _____
6. _____
7. _____
8. _____
9. _____
10. _____
11. _____
12. _____
13. _____
14. _____
15. _____
16. _____
17. _____
18. _____
19. _____
20. _____

SPELLING WORDS

1. quiet
2. trial
3. fuel
4. poem
5. diet
6. nucleus
7. cruel
8. Indian
9. fluid
10. violin
11. museum
12. dial
13. ruin
14. influence
15. triumph
16. violent
17. theater
18. liar
19. leotard
20. koala

Practice Book
Distant Voyages

© Harcourt

Name _____

▶ **Read the Vocabulary Words. Then write the Vocabulary Word that best completes each sentence.**

guarantee	distinguished	stumps	misleading
indebted	interpreter	suffrage	anthem

1. The _____ translated the President's speech into Japanese.

2. The President said he was proud of the Nineteenth Amendment to the United States Constitution, which granted _____ to women.

3. The United States wants to _____ everyone's right to vote.

4. The well-known and _____ panel of world leaders applauded.

5. Our national _____, "The Star-Spangled Banner," was written by Francis Scott Key.

6. All Americans are _____ to the brave people who helped build the nation.

7. _____ news stories about figures from American history should be ignored.

8. The question, "Who is the most important American?" _____ me every time.

▶ **Write the Vocabulary Word that fits in each web.**

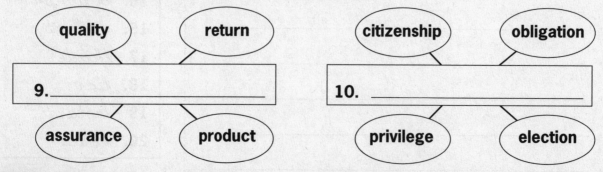

quality   return

9. _____

assurance   product

citizenship   obligation

10. _____

privilege   election

TRY THIS! Write a paragraph about a problem that *stumped* you. Use two of the Vocabulary Words.

118

Practice Book
Distant Voyages

Name _____

▶ **Read the paragraph. Then circle the letter of the best answer to each question.**

When Elizabeth Cady Stanton spoke at the Seneca Falls Convention in 1848, she wanted people to accept the idea of suffrage for women. There was much opposition and heated discussion following her speech. However, Elizabeth was greatly relieved and joyful, because she learned there were others who agreed with her. Outside the convention, people were outraged by the idea of suffrage for women. The speech caused a movement to begin. However, the goal did not become reality for another 72 years.

1 Why did Elizabeth give her speech at the convention?

A She wanted the people to stage a protest march.

B She wanted to be known as a public speaker.

C She wanted people to leave the convention.

D She wanted people to accept the idea that women should have the right to vote.

> **Tip**
> Elizabeth's motive is presented in the topic sentence of this paragraph.

2 Which of the following was NOT an effect of Elizabeth's speech?

F support from some people

G outrage from some people

H suffrage for women taking effect immediately

J setting the idea of suffrage for women in motion

> **Tip**
> Reread the details that support the topic sentence. Which answer choice is NOT one of those details?

3 It took 72 years for the idea to become reality because

A Elizabeth wanted it that way.

B many women supported her.

C Elizabeth did not express her views clearly.

D it took that long to change public opinion.

> **Tip**
> Based on what you learned in the paragraph, which statement seems most likely to be true?

© Harcourt

SCHOOL-HOME CONNECTION Discuss a current news story with your child. Focus on what might have caused the events in the story.

Practice Book
Distant Voyages

Name _____

Skill Reminder • A **contraction** is the shortened form of two words. An **apostrophe** takes the place of the letters left out. • A word that has *no* or *not* in its meaning is called a **negative**. Use only one negative in a sentence.

▶ **In the blank provided, write the correct contraction for the underlined words.**

1. <u>You have</u> probably heard about Elizabeth Cady Stanton's crusade for women's

   rights. _____

2. Women <u>could not</u> vote before 1921. _____

3. Stanton <u>did not</u> let that keep her from running for Congress in 1868.

   _____

4. <u>She would</u> have won if women had been able to vote. _____

▶ **Rewrite these sentences using the correct word in parentheses ( ).**

5. **(Its, It's)** remarkable that the panel had difficulty identifying the guests.

   _____

   _____

6. "I thought there **(was, wasn't)** no one who could fool me," said one panel member.

   _____

   _____

7. At the end of the game, there **(were, weren't)** no points scored by the panel.

   _____

   _____

8. The panel had never been stumped by **(anybody, nobody)** before.

   _____

   _____

 TRY THIS! Write five sentences about an American you admire. Use contractions and negatives.

© Harcourt

Name _____

Skill Reminder A **contraction** is a shortened form of two combined words. An apostrophe is used in place of the missing letter or letters.

▶ Fold the paper along the dotted line. As each spelling word is read aloud, write it in the blank. Then unfold your paper, and check your work. Practice spelling any words you missed.

1. _____

2. _____

3. _____

4. _____

5. _____

6. _____

7. _____

8. _____

9. _____

10. _____

11. _____

12. _____

13. _____

14. _____

15. _____

16. _____

17. _____

18. _____

19. _____

20. _____

SPELLING WORDS

1. he's
2. couldn't
3. she'll
4. doesn't
5. we'd
6. that's
7. hadn't
8. shouldn't
9. how's
10. weren't
11. there's
12. wouldn't
13. what's
14. where's
15. aren't
16. here's
17. they'll
18. we'll
19. you'd
20. he'd

Practice Book
Distant Voyages

121

Name _____

▶ **Read the Vocabulary Words. Then write the Vocabulary Word that best completes each sentence.**

edition	suspended	honors	contraption	repeal	treaty

1. The wind kept Ben's kite _____ in the air.

2. His odd _____ turned out to be a great invention.

3. Many ideas appeared in the first

_____ of his book.

4. One of his ideas was to _____ unfair taxes.

5. Another idea was to write a peace _____ to stop the war.

6. All the _____ for these great ideas go to Ben.

▶ **Write the Vocabulary Word that best completes each analogy.**

7. *Jogging* is to *running* as *dangled* is to _____.

8. *Start* is to *finish* as *pass* is to _____.

9. *Law* is to *order* as _____ is to *peace*.

10. *Actions* are to *deeds* as *awards* are to _____.

11. *Author* is to *book* as *inventor* is to _____.

12. *Magazine* is to *issue* as *book* is to _____.

TRY THIS! Think of a book title that includes one or two Vocabulary Words. Draw a book cover to go with your title. Write the title on your drawing.

© Harcourt

Name _____

▶ **Read the paragraph. Then circle the letter of the best answer to each question.**

In 1782 the ordeal of fighting for American independence was nearly over. However, the battle was still going on in New York. The army there desperately needed more soldiers. A young woman named Deborah Sampson heard about this. She could think of nothing but independence and freedom, so she made a suit of men's clothing, tied her hair in the men's fashion of the time, and volunteered for the army. She felt smug about finally being able to help her country.

1 Which idea does the word *ordeal* express?

A Achieving American independence was time-consuming.

B Achieving American independence was somewhat difficult.

C American independence was not achieved.

D Achieving American independence was very difficult.

💡 **Tip**

Which answer choice tells what the writer must have been thinking to call the war for independence not just a *struggle* but an *ordeal*?

2 Which idea does the word *volunteered* express?

F Deborah joined the army, but she did not feel very strongly about it.

G Deborah willingly and gladly went into the army.

H Deborah was forced into the army.

J Deborah enlisted in the army, but it wasn't her first choice.

💡 **Tip**

Look in the passage for Deborah's feelings about the Revolution. How does the word *volunteered* fit her feelings?

3 To express a more positive connotation, which word should the writer substitute for *smug*?

A self-satisfied

B thrilled

C content

D self-important

💡 **Tip**

Consider what you know about Deborah. Which answer choice would come closest to expressing her feelings?

SCHOOL-HOME CONNECTION Ask your child to substitute a few words in a magazine ad with words that have similar meanings but more negative feelings. Discuss how the new words change the meaning of the ad.

123

© Harcourt

Skill Reminder • An **adverb** is a word that describes a verb, an adjective, or another adverb. • An adverb tells how, when, where, or to what extent. Many adverbs that tell how end in *-ly*.

▶ Underline the adverb in each sentence. Draw an arrow to the word it describes. Then write *verb* or *adjective* to tell the kind of word the adverb describes.

1. The British firmly refused to repeal the tax. _____

2. Ben Franklin soon realized that war was coming. _____

3. "This law is very unfair," Franklin said. _____

4. He told the colonists, "We will fight the British everywhere." _____

5. The colonists were quite brave. _____

▶ Use the information in parentheses ( ) to help you complete each sentence. Choose from the adverbs in the following list.

extremely	sometimes	closely

6. _____ a person's eyesight needs correcting. **(when)**

7. Ben Franklin was _____ clever. **(to what extent)**

8. He examined the problem _____ and invented bifocal lenses. **(how)**

 TRY THIS! Write a short paragraph about an event or a person in history. Use at least four adverbs in your paragraph. Underline all the adverbs you use.

© Harcourt

Skill Reminder • The spelling and pronunciation of a word often change when a related word is formed. • For words ending in e, a long vowel often becomes a short vowel in the related word.

▶ Fold the paper along the dotted line. As each spelling word is read aloud, write it in the blank. Then unfold your paper, and check your work. Practice spelling any words you missed.

1. _____
2. _____
3. _____
4. _____
5. _____
6. _____
7. _____
8. _____
9. _____
10. _____
11. _____
12. _____
13. _____
14. _____
15. _____
16. _____
17. _____
18. _____
19. _____
20. _____

SPELLING WORDS

1. describe
2. description
3. nature
4. natural
5. televise
6. television
7. apply
8. application
9. compete
10. competition
11. divide
12. division
13. beauty
14. beautiful
15. collide
16. collision
17. multiply
18. multiplication
19. bounty
20. bountiful

Practice Book
Distant Voyages

Name _____

▶ **Read the Vocabulary Words. Write the Vocabulary Word that best completes each sentence.**

| profusely | ordeal | terrain | dismal | peril | esteem |

Meriwether Lewis and William Clark headed west in 1804.

They traveled over a **(1)** _____ of flat
plains and high mountains. The long, dangerous trip

was an **(2)** _____. The weather

was sometimes **(3)** _____,
changing from gray skies to cold rain.

The **(4)** _____ of exploring
uncharted, unknown country was great. When he began
the trip, Lewis wrote about his feelings in his journal, "I . . . **(5)** _____
this moment of my departure as among the most happy of my life." At the end,

both explorers were **(6)** _____ thankful that nearly all of their
group returned safely.

▶ **Read each word. Write the Vocabulary Word with nearly the same meaning.**

7. gloomy _____

8. countryside _____

9. danger _____

10. trial _____

11. honor _____

12. freely _____

TRY THIS!
Look at items 7–12. Write one sentence for each item. Use both words from each item in your sentences.

© Harcourt

126

Name _____

▶ **Read the paragraph. Then circle the letter of the best answer to each question.**

President Jefferson was interested in science. He wanted to know about the western land of the United States, so he asked Congress to send explorers into the unknown territory. Congress agreed. Jefferson hoped the expedition would gather information about new plants and animals. However, Congress wanted the expedition to open new lands for development. Although Jefferson's two amateur scientists, Lewis and Clark, collected a lot of information, the most important result of their journey was that it inspired others to travel west.

1 What caused Jefferson to send Lewis and Clark west?

A He thought they deserved a vacation.

B He hoped they would find new land for development.

C He wanted to know about the plants and animals in the West.

D He wanted to spend Congress's money.

> 💡 **Tip**
> Eliminate answers that make no sense.

2 Why did Congress agree to western exploration?

F The members of Congress were interested in plants and animals.

G Congress liked Jefferson.

H Congress wanted to develop new land.

J Congress thought that Lewis and Clark were good scientists.

> 💡 **Tip**
> Look for the sentence that tells what Congress wanted.

3 What was NOT an effect of the Lewis and Clark expedition?

A It inspired others to travel west.

B Lewis and Clark collected scientific information.

C Jefferson lost his interest in science.

D New lands were explored and opened for development.

> 💡 **Tip**
> Eliminate answer choices that you can find in the passage.

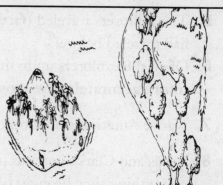

© Harcourt

SCHOOL-HOME CONNECTION Ask your child to tell you about cause-and-effect relationships around the home. For example, a switch is flipped (cause), and a light goes on (effect).

127

Practice Book
Distant Voyages

Name _____

> **Skill Reminder** • To compare one action with another, add *-er* to most short **adverbs.** Use the word *more* if the adverb has two or more syllables. • To compare one action with two or more other actions, add *-est* to most short **adverbs.** Use the word *most* if the adverb has two or more syllables.

▶ **Rewrite these sentences, using the correct form of the adverb in parentheses ( ).**

1. Of all the nations on Earth, the United States was growing _____. **(rapidly)**

_____

_____

2. Some volunteers responded _____ than others for the expedition. **(eagerly)**

_____

_____

3. Those who responded _____ of all were chosen to make the trip. **(fast)**

_____

_____

4. The men rowed _____ on the first day than they did on the second day. **(rapid)**

_____

_____

▶ **Complete these sentences by underlining the correct choice.**

5. The explorers traveled **(farther, farthest)** into the West than any U.S. expedition had traveled before.

6. Of all the explorers up to that time, Lewis and Clark mapped the West **(more accurately, the most accurately).**

7. Native Americans built canoes **(skillfully, more skillfully)** than the explorers.

8. Lewis and Clark's journals provided **(more valuable, the most valuable)** information of anything they brought back.

© Harcourt

128

Practice Book
Distant Voyages

Name _____

Skill Reminder   When spelling a three-syllable word, listen to
the vowel sound in each syllable. Then spell the word one syllable
at a time. Remember that a schwa sound (/ə/) can be spelled with any vowel.

▶ Fold the paper along the dotted line. As each spelling word is read aloud, write it
   in the blank. Then unfold your paper, and check your work. Practice spelling any
   words you missed.

1. _____
2. _____
3. _____
4. _____
5. _____
6. _____
7. _____
8. _____
9. _____
10. _____
11. _____
12. _____
13. _____
14. _____
15. _____
16. _____
17. _____
18. _____
19. _____
20. _____

SPELLING WORDS

1. industry
2. buffalo
3. exciting
4. terrible
5. electric
6. dangerous
7. exercise
8. horizon
9. favorite
10. library
11. substitute
12. typical
13. dinosaur
14. curious
15. average
16. period
17. amazement
18. bicycle
19. conference
20. family

Practice Book
Distant Voyages

▶ As you read each sentence, use context clues to determine the meaning of the Vocabulary Word in dark print. Then write the Vocabulary Word that best completes each analogy.

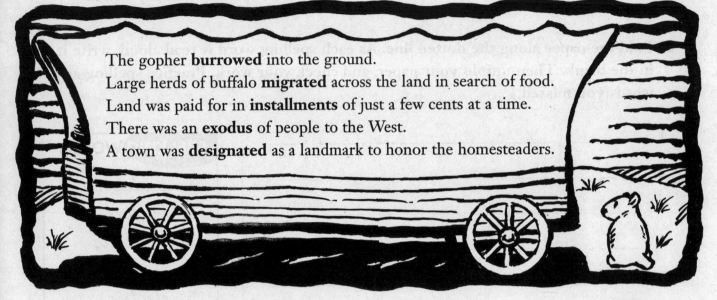

The gopher **burrowed** into the ground.
Large herds of buffalo **migrated** across the land in search of food.
Land was paid for in **installments** of just a few cents at a time.
There was an **exodus** of people to the West.
A town was **designated** as a landmark to honor the homesteaders.

1. *Whole* is to *parts* as *total* is to _____.

2. *Halted* is to *stayed* as *moved* is to _____.

3. *Flurry* is to *blizzard* as *departure* is to _____.

4. *Web* is to *wove* as *hole* is to _____.

5. *Purified* is to *refined* as *named* is to _____.

▶ Read each group of words. Cross out the word that does *not* belong. Then write the Vocabulary Word that best fits with the remaining words.

6.	tunneled	froze	groundhog	_____
7.	anonymous	chosen	selected	_____
8.	climate	exit	departure	_____
9.	traveled	journeyed	settled	_____
10.	regular	payments	detach	_____

TRY THIS! Suppose you were a pioneer, either in a past era of history or in a future time of exploration. Write a paragraph about your experience using at least three Vocabulary Words.

Name _____

▶ **Read the paragraph. Then circle the letter of the best answer to each question.**

Homesteading on the Great Plains required bravery and hard work. Land had to be cleared of rocks and grass before crops could be planted. Farmers needed a horse or mule and a plow to prepare the land. Settlers needed seeds for planting and enough food to eat until harvest time. Since there were no stores, pioneers learned to brew teas from wild grasses and to make their own soap and shampoo from the yucca plant. Most of all, homesteaders needed a home to protect them from the weather. Constructing a dwelling of sod or mud adobe was their highest priority.

1 Which is the best summary of this passage?

 A Settlers needed to make things like soap and shampoo because there were no stores.

 B Settlers' homes were made of sod or adobe.

 C Land had to be cleared of rocks and grass.

 D Settlers worked hard to till and farm the land and build their homes.

> **Tip**
> A summary is a brief statement that retells the most important ideas of a passage.

2 Which is the best paraphrase of the first sentence?

 F The Great Plains was not a place for the strong-willed.

 G Settlers on the Great Plains had to have courage and had to work hard.

 H Homesteading was rarely done on the Great Plains.

 J Homesteading on the Great Plains required persistence and hard work.

> **Tip**
> Eliminate the choices that have completely different meanings.

3 Which is the best paraphrase for the last sentence?

 A Dwellings were constructed of sod or mud adobe.

 B Building a sod or mud adobe home was their most important task.

 C Constructing a dwelling of sod or mud adobe was their highest priority.

 D Using mud or sod adobe was the most important thing.

> **Tip**
> Eliminate the choice that restates the sentence exactly. This is not a paraphrase.

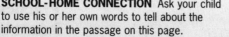 **SCHOOL-HOME CONNECTION** Ask your child to use his or her own words to tell about the information in the passage on this page.

 131

Practice Book
Distant Voyages

© Harcourt

Name _____

▶ **Read the information in each chart or graph. Then answer the questions.**

Train Number 303 Daily Hours of Operation			Distance (in miles)
9:20 A.M.	Depart	Chicago, IL	0
12:15 P.M. 12:38 P.M.	Arrive Depart	Springfield, IL	185
3:05 P.M. 3:30 P.M.	Arrive Depart	St. Louis, MO	284
9:10 P.M.	Arrive	Kansas City, MO	567

1. How is the information in the train schedule organized?

A alphabetically

B by time

C by date

2. What time does the train arrive in Kansas City, Missouri?

_____

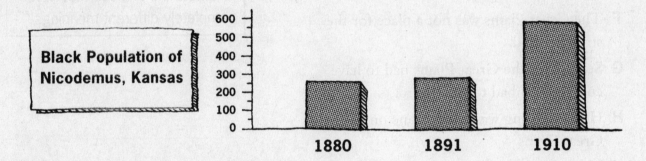

Black Population of Nicodemus, Kansas

600 500 400 300 200 100 0

1880   1891   1910

3. How is the population information organized?

A alphabetically

B by year, in a graph

C most important to least important

4. What was the population of Nicodemus in 1910? _____

5. If you wanted to list the names of all the people in Nicodemus in 1910, what are two

ways you could organize your list? _____

Practice Book
Distant Voyages

© Harcourt

Name _____

Skill Reminder • **A preposition** tells the relationship of a noun or pronoun to another word in the sentence. • The noun or pronoun that follows a preposition is the **object of the preposition.** • **A prepositional phrase** is made up of a preposition, the object of the preposition, and the words in between.

▶ Underline the prepositional phrase. Write the preposition and its object on the line.

1. Homesteaders sometimes built log homes on the prairie land. _____

2. In prairie states, the grass was very tall. _____

3. The sod under the tough grass could be cut into bricks. _____

4. The homesteaders stacked the bricks into the shape of a house. _____

▶ Rewrite these sentences, adding a preposition to fill each blank.

5. Winters _____ northern states can be very cold. _____

_____

6. Temperatures sometimes fall _____ zero degrees. _____

_____

7. Some homesteaders dug homes _____ the earth. _____

_____

8. Small animals were brought inside _____ the winter. _____

_____

TRY THIS! Write two more sentences about homesteaders. Include prepositional phrases in your sentences. Underline the prepositional phrases that you use.

Practice Book
Distant Voyages

Skill Reminder   **Many English words come from Spanish.**

▶ Fold the paper along the dotted line. As each spelling word is read aloud, write it in the blank. Then unfold your paper, and check your work. Practice spelling any words you missed.

1. _____

2. _____

3. _____

4. _____

5. _____

6. _____

7. _____

8. _____

9. _____

10. _____

11. _____

12. _____

13. _____

14. _____

15. _____

16. _____

17. _____

18. _____

19. _____

20. _____

SPELLING WORDS

1. canyon
2. tornado
3. breeze
4. cafeteria
5. coyote
6. tomato
7. barbecue
8. mosquito
9. plaza
10. pueblo
11. chili
12. alligator
13. rodeo
14. patio
15. bonanza
16. avocado
17. mesa
18. burro
19. enchilada
20. burrito

© Harcourt

Practice Book
Distant Voyages

Skills and Strategies Index

Skills and Strategies Index

LITERARY RESPONSE AND ANALYSIS

SPELLING

RESEARCH AND INFORMATION SKILLS

VOCABULARY

· T R O P H I E S ·

End-of-Selection Tests

Grade 5

The Hot and Cold Summer

Directions: For items 1–18, fill in the circle in front of the correct answer. For items 19–20, write the answer.

Vocabulary

1. You wouldn't believe all the _____ in the room when a bird flew in the window.
   - Ⓐ souvenir
   - Ⓑ incredible
   - Ⓒ commotion
   - Ⓓ exhausted

2. Louie made a _____ that he would help the team in whatever way he could.
   - Ⓐ vow
   - Ⓑ close
   - Ⓒ vane
   - Ⓓ learn

3. When we were on vacation, each of us bought one _____ .
   - Ⓐ authority
   - Ⓑ souvenir
   - Ⓒ remember
   - Ⓓ incredible

4. An _____ on Egyptian art visited our classroom and told us about the pyramids.
   - Ⓐ exhausted
   - Ⓑ authority
   - Ⓒ incredible
   - Ⓓ enrich

5. The gymnast performed an _____ routine when she won first place.
   - Ⓐ authority
   - Ⓑ examiner
   - Ⓒ incredible
   - Ⓓ earth

6. Because the players put forth such effort, they are now _____ .
   - Ⓐ exhausted
   - Ⓑ incredible
   - Ⓒ commotion
   - Ⓓ illustrated

Comprehension

7. This selection is realistic fiction because _____ .
   - (A) it is about a person's life
   - (B) the story has a beginning, middle, and end
   - (C) there is conflict between good and evil
   - (D) the setting and characters could be real

8. At the beginning of the story, Rory and Derek do not want to meet Lucette because they _____ .
   - (A) do not care that she has said her first words
   - (B) do not like girls
   - (C) are afraid of her
   - (D) do not like parrots

9. How is Edna related to one of the other children?
   - (A) She is Bolivia's cousin.
   - (B) She is Rory's sister.
   - (C) She is Lucette's cousin.
   - (D) She is Derek's sister.

10. The boys do not want to talk to Bolivia, so they _____ .
    - (A) take turns cooking on the grill
    - (B) pay attention to Edna
    - (C) keep stuffing food into their mouths
    - (D) joke about the turkey burgers

11. Mr. Dunn wants Rory to _____ .
    - (A) eat more burgers and potato salad
    - (B) talk to Edna
    - (C) help him serve the food
    - (D) tell Bolivia about Woodside

12. All the following are clues that make the boys think Lucette is a baby **except** _____ .
   (A) Bolivia plays "This little piggy went to market"
   (B) Lucette says her first word to Mrs. Golding
   (C) Bolivia cannot bring Lucette to the barbecue because the smoke might bother her
   (D) Lucette knows ten words

13. Why does Rory think that girls really have no idea what boys like to do?
   (A) Bolivia suggests that the boys play with Lucette.
   (B) Bolivia wants to tell the boys all about her travels.
   (C) Edna and Lucette want to play with Rory and Derek.
   (D) Bolivia plays "This little piggy went to market" with Edna.

14. When Rory sees Bolivia go through the hedge to the back of the house, he thinks that she _____ .
   (A) is angry and has left the party
   (B) is going to get Lucette
   (C) will return with pictures of her trip
   (D) knows the boys don't want her around

15. What does Rory have as a souvenir of the first afternoon he hid from Bolivia?
   (A) a sprout from a sandwich
   (B) a burned hot dog
   (C) a card for the swimming pool
   (D) a movie stub

16. Why does the summer stretch endlessly before the boys?
   (A) because it is only June
   (B) because school has just gotten out
   (C) because it will be a long time before Bolivia leaves Woodside
   (D) because they have nothing to do

17. Why isn't it only their vow of silence that keeps Rory and Derek from admitting that they thought Lucette was a baby?

(A) Rory and Derek think that Bolivia is playing a joke on them.

(B) The boys are embarrassed and cannot admit they made a mistake.

(C) The boys are silent because they do not like Lucette.

(D) The boys really dislike Bolivia.

18. Why does Derek forget that he promised never to speak to Bolivia?

(A) because Bolivia and Edna are having a good time

(B) because the fire department comes to rescue Lucette

(C) because Rory starts talking to her

(D) because Lucette is so interesting

19. How do Rory and Derek feel when they think Lucette is a baby who fell out of a window? after they learn that Lucette is a parrot in a tree?

_____

_____

_____

_____

_____

_____

20. What does Rory suspect?

_____

_____

_____

_____

_____

Sees Behind Trees

Directions: For items 1–18, fill in the circle in front of the correct answer. For items 19–20, write the answer.

Vocabulary

1. The students were told to stop giggling and to _____ themselves before the guest speaker arrived.
   - (A) compose
   - (B) sternly
   - (C) tread
   - (D) quiver

2. Tell me exactly what happened, and do not _____ the facts.
   - (A) incredible
   - (B) exaggerate
   - (C) humble
   - (D) exhaust

3. Ray, an excellent marksman, pulled an arrow from his _____ .
   - (A) compose
   - (B) tread
   - (C) sternly
   - (D) quiver

4. The trees along the highway are covered with silvery _____ .
   - (A) tread
   - (B) compose
   - (C) moss
   - (D) loss

5. When my brother was late for dinner, my dad spoke to him _____ .
   - (A) authority
   - (B) exhausted
   - (C) slowly
   - (D) sternly

6. We heard the _____ of my uncle's boots as he walked across the porch.
   - (A) quiver
   - (B) tread
   - (C) compose
   - (D) exaggerate

Comprehension

7. What must happen before Walnut can have breakfast?
   - (A) He has to practice throwing moss into the air.
   - (B) He must make his bow ready to shoot.
   - (C) He has to make arrows to shoot.
   - (D) He must hit the target with a bow and arrow.

8. Walnut's mother is _____ .

Ⓐ very serious about teaching him to shoot with a bow and arrow

Ⓑ a good archer, so she wants him to be one

Ⓒ very gentle when she is teaching him to shoot

Ⓓ sure that her son will be a great archer

9. What does Brings the Deer say is the trick to being a good archer?

Ⓐ a good bow   Ⓑ practice

Ⓒ three fingers   Ⓓ closing your eyes

10. How does Brings the Deer discover Walnut's problem?

Ⓐ He asks Walnut to shoot an arrow.

Ⓑ He tells Walnut to look at the fireflies.

Ⓒ He asks Walnut to count his fingers.

Ⓓ He checks the string on Walnut's bow.

11. The story is based on the fact that Walnut is _____ .

Ⓐ not able to see well

Ⓑ not old enough to hunt

Ⓒ very hungry

Ⓓ like his uncle

12. Why does Walnut's mother tie a sash around his eyes when they sit in the forest?

Ⓐ She wants to make it harder for him to hit the target.

Ⓑ Brings the Deer advises her to try a new method.

Ⓒ She wants Walnut to use his sense of hearing to "see."

Ⓓ Walnut can see through a sash around his eyes.

13. Walnut is discouraged about learning to shoot, but _____ .

Ⓐ he doesn't care if he ever learns how to shoot

Ⓑ it doesn't matter because Brings the Deer is the best archer in the family

Ⓒ he can "see" things his mother cannot

Ⓓ he asks his dad to teach him how to shoot

© Harcourt

14. Why doesn't Walnut want to go to the shooting contest?
Ⓐ because Brings the Deer will be ashamed of him
Ⓑ because he has not learned to shoot
Ⓒ because his father will not come to see him
Ⓓ because he wants his mother to give him breakfast first

15. The weroance, the most important person in the tribe, _____ .
Ⓐ has a shrill voice that scares everyone
Ⓑ conducts the fishing contest
Ⓒ teaches bow and arrow skills
Ⓓ is the expert on hunting

16. Why does the weroance have the new contest first?
Ⓐ to keep Walnut from failing the bow and arrow contest
Ⓑ to see if Gray Fire is nearby
Ⓒ to prevent something bad from happening
Ⓓ to show that Walnut's skills are important

17. The weroance's brother is named Gray Fire because he _____ .
Ⓐ has difficulty climbing hills
Ⓑ walks quietly and passes through places like smoke
Ⓒ is light on his feet, although he limps
Ⓓ likes to build big, smoky fires

18. This selection is most like historical fiction because the selection is _____ .
Ⓐ set in the past and is about events that might have happened
Ⓑ set in modern times and is about events that might have happened
Ⓒ filled with suspense
Ⓓ not realistic and has characters that could not exist

19. How does wearing the sash help Walnut win the contest?

_____

_____

_____

_____

_____

_____

_____

_____

_____

20. Why does Walnut receive the name Sees Behind Trees?

_____

_____

_____

_____

_____

_____

_____

_____

_____

_____

© Harcourt

Yang the Third and Her Impossible Family

Directions: For items 1–18, fill in the circle in front of the correct answer. For items 19–20, write the answer.

Vocabulary

1. I would never have won the singing award if my _____ had not played so well.
   - (A) audition
   - (B) sonata
   - (C) accompanist
   - (D) grimaced

2. Do you plan to _____ for the lead role in the play?
   - (A) sonata
   - (B) audition
   - (C) simultaneously
   - (D) tread

3. Can you juggle three balls _____?
   - (A) grimaced
   - (B) authority
   - (C) simultaneously
   - (D) accompanist

4. During last evening's concert, the orchestra played a Mozart _____ beautifully.
   - (A) commotion
   - (B) audition
   - (C) compose
   - (D) sonata

5. The singers requested piano music as their _____ .
   - (A) accompaniment
   - (B) souvenir
   - (C) audition
   - (D) enrollment

6. Frank _____ when he heard the teacher's nail scrape on the chalkboard.
   - (A) exhausted
   - (B) simultaneously
   - (C) glowed
   - (D) grimaced

Comprehension

7. This selection is most like _____ .

   Ⓐ a poem   Ⓑ realistic fiction

   Ⓒ historical fiction   Ⓓ a biography

8. What is Holly's problem?

   Ⓐ Holly's mother cannot drive her to rehearsal.

   Ⓑ Her accompanist is sick.

   Ⓒ Mary can't play the cello.

   Ⓓ Holly hasn't practiced enough.

9. To help Holly, Mary suggests that _____ .

   Ⓐ she play her cello to accompany Holly

   Ⓑ Mrs. Hanson be the accompanist

   Ⓒ her mother accompany Holly

   Ⓓ Holly can practice every day at her house

10. Who is telling the story?

   Ⓐ Mrs. Hanson   Ⓑ Holly

   Ⓒ Kim   Ⓓ Mary

11. Unlike Holly, Mary feels that being in the Junior Chamber Orchestra would be _____ .

   Ⓐ boring   Ⓑ wonderful

   Ⓒ time-consuming   Ⓓ expensive

12. What is more important to Holly than getting into the Junior Chamber Orchestra?

   Ⓐ raising purebred dogs   Ⓑ going to camp

   Ⓒ being in a play   Ⓓ practicing with friends

13. Mary hopes that if her mother plays the piano for Holly, the Hansons will show her mother more _____ .

   Ⓐ respect   Ⓑ authority

   Ⓒ style   Ⓓ commotion

© Harcourt

14. Mrs. Sylvester thinks cats are _____ .

  Ⓐ friendly animals   Ⓑ nicer than her dog

  Ⓒ noisier than dogs   Ⓓ stuck up

15. "To walk across the room, you had to negotiate carefully between piles." In this story, *negotiate* means to _____ .

  Ⓐ talk about something to get an agreement

  Ⓑ travel successfully

  Ⓒ jump from place to place

  Ⓓ look at, from a distance

16. When Holly practices with Mrs. Yang, everyone can see that Holly _____ .

  Ⓐ loves to play her viola

  Ⓑ will win a place in the orchestra

  Ⓒ doesn't have her heart in playing

  Ⓓ is thinking about dogs

17. Mrs. Yang keeps saying she is not really very good because _____ .

  Ⓐ she plays without feeling

  Ⓑ she makes several mistakes

  Ⓒ the piano needs tuning

  Ⓓ it is rude for a Chinese person to agree with a compliment

18. Mary speaks up when Mrs. Hanson and Holly laugh at her family because _____ .

  Ⓐ she thinks that they are making fun of her family

  Ⓑ she thinks that they should be ashamed of their laughing

  Ⓒ they are wrong about her mother's playing

  Ⓓ Holly probably makes mistakes when she is playing

© Harcourt

19. Mrs. Hanson suddenly begins to laugh and sing "Yes! We have no bananas!" when

_____

_____

_____

_____

_____

_____

_____

_____

20. Mary is ashamed because her family doesn't try harder to learn American ways. What does she learn about this attitude by the end of the story?

_____

_____

_____

_____

_____

_____

_____

_____

Dear Mrs. Parks

Directions: For items 1–18, fill in the circle in front of the correct answer. For items 19–20, write the answer.

Vocabulary

1. I owe letters to so many people that I'm not sure how to catch up on my _____ .
   - Ⓐ correspondence
   - Ⓑ potential
   - Ⓒ counsel
   - Ⓓ ridiculed

2. His brave actions will _____ others to have courage also.
   - Ⓐ counsel
   - Ⓑ dignity
   - Ⓒ inspire
   - Ⓓ audition

3. She carried herself with pride and _____ , knowing she had behaved with honor.
   - Ⓐ inspire
   - Ⓑ mentor
   - Ⓒ inspection
   - Ⓓ dignity

4. Some students _____ the younger children for the way they dressed.
   - Ⓐ sternly
   - Ⓑ correspondence
   - Ⓒ ridiculed
   - Ⓓ potential

5. Mary Lee has the _____ to be a great leader.
   - Ⓐ inspire
   - Ⓑ mentor
   - Ⓒ potential
   - Ⓓ accompanist

6. My brother's teachers will _____ him about the classes he will take at middle school.
   - Ⓐ counsel
   - Ⓑ dignity
   - Ⓒ compare
   - Ⓓ authority

7. My sister feels it is important to find a good _____, since this is her first real job.
   - Ⓐ potential
   - Ⓑ mentor
   - Ⓒ inspire
   - Ⓓ accompanist

Comprehension

8. What does Mrs. Parks tell Jimmy about asking questions?

   Ⓐ He can learn by listening to other people's questions.

   Ⓑ A person should never be afraid to admit not knowing something.

   Ⓒ Asking questions does not help people solve their problems.

   Ⓓ Never let anyone know if you don't know something.

9. What does Mrs. Parks believe is the greatest value of asking questions?

   Ⓐ Asking questions helps you learn things.

   Ⓑ Asking questions keeps people from being afraid.

   Ⓒ The answers tell you exactly what to do.

   Ⓓ Asking questions helps you make better choices in life.

10. What does Mrs. Parks mean when she tells Richard to "keep an open mind"?

   Ⓐ His dad is wrong.

   Ⓑ He should continue to learn throughout his life.

   Ⓒ He should act as though he knows something, even if he doesn't.

   Ⓓ He ought to learn as much as he can about computers.

11. Mrs. Parks's message to students is "Work hard, do not be discouraged, and in everything you do, _____ ."

   Ⓐ try to do your best

   Ⓑ express your gifts

   Ⓒ achieve your potential

   Ⓓ start leading

12. Why does Mrs. Parks say, "We are all leaders of something in life"?

   Ⓐ School can make leaders of everyone.

   Ⓑ Mrs. Parks believes that we all have gifts or talents.

   Ⓒ Mrs. Parks believes in hard work.

   Ⓓ Mrs. Parks says people should never be afraid of being ridiculed.

13. What does Rosa Parks learn from her grandmother?

Ⓐ math, science, and literature

Ⓑ to care for sickly people

Ⓒ the importance of personal dignity

Ⓓ how to cook and do housework

14. Grandmothers tell stories from the past to inspire you, to help you learn from mistakes of the past, and to _____ .

Ⓐ keep you out of trouble

Ⓑ show you how to do things

Ⓒ help you learn a new language

Ⓓ keep history alive

15. According to Mrs. Parks, what can your grandmothers' stories do for you?

Ⓐ teach you how to have a good time

Ⓑ help you work for freedom

Ⓒ give you courage, faith, and a willingness to sacrifice

Ⓓ prepare you to take your place in the world of tomorrow

16. Which best describes Rosa Parks?

Ⓐ She is involved in new ideas and interests.

Ⓑ She is no longer interested in other people.

Ⓒ She is discouraged about America's future.

Ⓓ She is tired and very old.

17. According to Mrs. Parks, one way a person can make a difference in the world is by _____ .

Ⓐ choosing a technical job

Ⓑ doing what he or she can do for others

Ⓒ keeping to herself or himself and not helping others

Ⓓ not working with a community group

A15

18. Why did the author help Mrs. Parks publish her letters?

- Ⓐ to get people to fight against homelessness
- Ⓑ to demonstrate the importance of grandmothers
- Ⓒ to show the kind of person Mrs. Parks is
- Ⓓ to support exercise activities for older people

19. Why is Mrs. Parks proud to be an American?

_____

_____

_____

_____

_____

_____

_____

_____

20. What does Mrs. Parks think is the duty of every American?

_____

_____

_____

_____

_____

_____

_____

_____

Directions: For items 1–18, fill in the circle in front of the correct answer.
For items 19–20, write the answer.

Vocabulary

1. The horse swam to shore after it _____ into the river.
   - Ⓐ mocking
   - Ⓑ determination
   - Ⓒ plunged
   - Ⓓ ravine

2. Because of her _____ and hard work, Lisa was named student of the year.
   - Ⓐ determination
   - Ⓑ revolution
   - Ⓒ mocking
   - Ⓓ dimension

3. The mayor offered _____ to the people who lost their homes in the fire.
   - Ⓐ mentor
   - Ⓑ accompanist
   - Ⓒ commotion
   - Ⓓ condolences

4. Many people fought hard for freedom in the _____ .
   - Ⓐ revolution
   - Ⓑ mocking
   - Ⓒ tradition
   - Ⓓ concrete

5. A small pond has formed at the bottom of the _____ .
   - Ⓐ plunged
   - Ⓑ potential
   - Ⓒ reside
   - Ⓓ ravine

6. The debater for the other team answered the question in a _____ tone.
   - Ⓐ mocking
   - Ⓑ determination
   - Ⓒ condolences
   - Ⓓ crying

Comprehension

7. According to this selection, a revolution began about 1910 because _____ .
   - Ⓐ land had been stolen from the campesinos
   - Ⓑ several villagers went to Guadalajara with Father
   - Ⓒ Father fell into a ravine that year
   - Ⓓ Father was taking a trip to Guadalajara

8. Why does Father tell Mother to take the children and leave their village?
   - (A) He knows Pancho Villa is coming and will kill them.
   - (B) He thinks Mexico is not a good place to raise children.
   - (C) He predicts the revolution and thinks they will not be safe.
   - (D) He thinks they can earn more money in California.

9. Pancho Villa is called the Robin Hood of Mexico because he is _____ .
   - (A) leading a revolution in Mexico
   - (B) trying to return the land to the people
   - (C) a bandit and robber
   - (D) a friend of Porfirio Diaz

10. Why was Elena so worried when she could not find her son at home?
    - (A) He left an open book on his bed.
    - (B) He was on the roof.
    - (C) She was afraid he would be forced into the army.
    - (D) She has great courage and determination.

11. The horses are moved into the kitchen because _____ .
    - (A) the barn is cold
    - (B) soldiers would think the family had left
    - (C) soldiers might steal the horses
    - (D) Esteban was in the kitchen

12. Why does the family go to San Francisco when they first leave Mexico?
    - (A) The barrio is there.
    - (B) Many Mexicans live there.
    - (C) It was a famous place.
    - (D) Cousin Trinidad invited them to come.

13. After the family left San Francisco, they moved to _____ .
    - (A) Los Angeles
    - (B) a Mexican village
    - (C) Santa Ana
    - (D) El Paso

Practice Book
Distant Voyages

14. In this selection, how does the mother support the family?

Ⓐ She becomes a teacher.

Ⓑ She opens a restaurant.

Ⓒ She runs a boarding house.

Ⓓ She works on a farm.

15. What does the storyteller mean by "I realized that Americans weren't 'they' anymore"?

Ⓐ Mother and some of the children returned to Mexico.

Ⓑ School was fun.

Ⓒ Her mother liked living in California.

Ⓓ She began to feel that her family belonged.

16. How does the storyteller learn about Father?

Ⓐ by reading about him in history books

Ⓑ looking at the sombreros he made

Ⓒ from stories Mother tells about him

Ⓓ from a visit to Mexico

17. This selection is most like _____ .

Ⓐ a poem

Ⓑ realistic fiction

Ⓒ historical fiction

Ⓓ a biography

18. The tone of this selection is best described as _____ .

Ⓐ apologetic

Ⓑ sad

Ⓒ angry

Ⓓ courageous

© Harcourt

19. Why does Mother tell the children their real job is to get an education?

_____

_____

_____

_____

_____

_____

_____

20. What does Mother say that makes you think she does not mind having to work hard?

_____

_____

_____

_____

_____

_____

_____

_____

_____

We'll Never Forget You, Roberto Clemente

Directions: For items 1–18, fill in the circle in front of the correct answer. For items 19–20, write the answer.

Vocabulary

1. He was an _____ pilot who handled the plane with skill and confidence.
   - (A) artificial
   - (B) ace
   - (C) error
   - (D) inspire

2. We _____ the new fountain to a teacher who taught at our school for thirty years.
   - (A) plunged
   - (B) artificial
   - (C) ridiculed
   - (D) dedicated

3. Kim, our best hitter, is fourth in the team's batting _____ .
   - (A) lineup
   - (B) error
   - (C) control tower
   - (D) ballplayer

4. When the catcher dropped the ball, it was called an _____ .
   - (A) artificial
   - (B) error
   - (C) inspire
   - (D) ace

5. The pilot radioed the _____ for permission to land the plane.
   - (A) control tower
   - (B) dedicated
   - (C) lineup
   - (D) potential

6. After being in a bad car accident, the man needed an _____ leg.
   - (A) ace
   - (B) error
   - (C) authority
   - (D) artificial

Practice Book
Distant Voyages

Comprehension

7. In 1972, Roberto Clemente wanted to be the 11th major league player
to _____ .

Ⓐ hit a home run
Ⓑ get into the major leagues
Ⓒ get into the Hall of Fame
Ⓓ get 3,000 hits

8. Clemente missed a lot of games during the 1972 season because
he _____ .

Ⓐ wasn't well or was injured
Ⓑ didn't want to play anymore
Ⓒ had no uniform
Ⓓ had lost interest in baseball

9. People didn't think Clemente could get 3,000 hits in the 1972 season
because _____ .

Ⓐ he was never up at bat
Ⓑ there weren't many games left in the season
Ⓒ it was raining almost every day
Ⓓ no fans were cheering

10. Why was Clemente taken out of the game after his 2,999th hit?

Ⓐ Everyone wanted him to make his 3,000th hit in front of the
hometown fans.
Ⓑ He was too tired to play the rest of the game.
Ⓒ The umpire threw him out of the game.
Ⓓ He wasn't hitting well at all.

11. The Pirates fans felt cheated when _____ .

Ⓐ Clemente stopped playing baseball
Ⓑ the other team booed Clemente
Ⓒ Clemente's hit was ruled an error
Ⓓ Clemente got hit number 3,000

12. Clemente got his 3,000th hit in a game against the _____ .

   Ⓐ Phillies   Ⓑ Yankees

   Ⓒ Pirates   Ⓓ Mets

13. Which terrible event occurred in Nicaragua in 1972?

   Ⓐ A flood destroyed the biggest city.

   Ⓑ An earthquake hit the biggest city.

   Ⓒ A tornado destroyed the smallest city.

   Ⓓ An earthquake hit the smallest city.

14. According to the selection, how did Clemente help a fourteen-year-old Nicaraguan boy?

   Ⓐ He took the boy to a Pirates game.

   Ⓑ He helped the boy get artificial legs.

   Ⓒ He helped the boy move to Puerto Rico.

   Ⓓ He gave the boy an autographed bat.

15. How was Clemente's father a role model for Roberto?

   Ⓐ His father taught him to help others in need.

   Ⓑ His father showed him how to hit fastballs.

   Ⓒ His father made him work very hard.

   Ⓓ His father sent him to the best schools.

16. Clemente helped get supplies to the people of Nicaragua because _____ .

   Ⓐ they asked him to help

   Ⓑ he had nothing to do in the United States

   Ⓒ his father told him to do it

   Ⓓ they had a disaster and needed help

17. This selection is most like _____ .

   Ⓐ an informational article

   Ⓑ a biography

   Ⓒ a personal diary

   Ⓓ a poem

18. The tone of this selection is best described as _____ .

Ⓐ apologetic   Ⓑ angry

Ⓒ courageous   Ⓓ admiring

19. Where was Roberto Clemente going when he died? Why was he going there?

_____

_____

_____

_____

_____

_____

_____

_____

20. How does the title of the story tell you that people valued Roberto Clemente as a person?

_____

_____

_____

_____

_____

_____

_____

_____

_____

_____

© Harcourt

Directions: For items 1–18, fill in the circle in front of the correct answer. For items 19–20, write the answer.

Vocabulary

1. When Dad went on vacation, he _____ the care of the animals on our farm to my brother.
   - Ⓐ plodded
   - Ⓑ plunged
   - Ⓒ entrusted
   - Ⓓ determined

2. Because of good weather and the farmer's hard work, the harvest will be _____ this year.
   - Ⓐ entrusted
   - Ⓑ bountiful
   - Ⓒ ridiculed
   - Ⓓ diligence

3. The postmaster _____ us that the package would be delivered in two days.
   - Ⓐ plodded
   - Ⓑ dedicated
   - Ⓒ assured
   - Ⓓ arrived

4. The candidate's _____ depended on the outcome of the election.
   - Ⓐ mocking
   - Ⓑ destiny
   - Ⓒ bountiful
   - Ⓓ detection

5. The old man _____ along the dirt road with slow, heavy steps.
   - Ⓐ plodded
   - Ⓑ entrusted
   - Ⓒ assured
   - Ⓓ glanced

6. The lawyer studied the terms of the contract with great _____ .
   - Ⓐ bountiful
   - Ⓑ destiny
   - Ⓒ entrusted
   - Ⓓ diligence

Comprehension

7. The stories in this selection are most like folktales because _____ .

  Ⓐ each story entertains and teaches a lesson

  Ⓑ the characters are animals that act like real people

  Ⓒ each story is set in a real place

  Ⓓ each story was told orally before it was written down

8. The Jade Emperor assigned the job of overseeing the earth to _____ .

  Ⓐ his youngest daughter

  Ⓑ his oldest daughter

  Ⓒ the palanquin bearers

  Ⓓ Tay Vuong Mau

9. How are the winter bearers and summer bearers of the palanquin different?

  Ⓐ Winter bearers are young and strong; summer bearers are old and tired.

  Ⓑ Summer bearers arrive early in the west; winter bearers arrive late.

  Ⓒ Winter bearers have gray beards, and the summer bearers are strong and muscular.

  Ⓓ There is a different number of bearers for each season.

10. In the selection "How the Moon Became Ivory," why do Earth people grow more tired each day?

  Ⓐ Working in the hot sun in the fields all day makes them tired.

  Ⓑ Earth people were not able to sleep in the bright, hot nights.

  Ⓒ Roosters slept in the day and crowed all night.

  Ⓓ Bearers were noisy as they carried the moon across the sky.

11. The sun discovers that the earth people _____ .

  Ⓐ are proud and selfish

  Ⓑ need time to rest

  Ⓒ are tired and lazy

  Ⓓ are afraid of darkness

© Harcourt

12. Tay Vuong Mau solves the earth people's problem by _____ .
   Ⓐ giving the moon a pot of ashes to put on her face and windows
   Ⓑ telling the sun not to shine as brightly
   Ⓒ telling the moon she is ugly and must hide her face
   Ⓓ making the heavenly bear her watchman

13. The wise woman tells Virtue to go to town because he _____ .
   Ⓐ has no parents
   Ⓑ wants to know his destiny
   Ⓒ hates being bored
   Ⓓ is not a good farmer

14. When the foreman tells Virtue that no one likes a braggart, Virtue _____ .
   Ⓐ apologizes and goes quickly to the back of the line
   Ⓑ says his name is Turnip
   Ⓒ starts a riot with the townspeople
   Ⓓ argues that it isn't bragging if you can do the task

15. Virtue picks up a cauldron in each hand. In this story, a *cauldron* is a _____ .
   Ⓐ bowl of rice
   Ⓑ huge kettle
   Ⓒ serving plate
   Ⓓ water jug

16. In the selection "Who Is Best?" what happens to the men on the seventh day?
   Ⓐ The men finish their job and the rich man gave them a party.
   Ⓑ They finish the job but are given no food.
   Ⓒ They do not finish the job but had a party.
   Ⓓ They watch the servant hide the food.

17. Mr. Panya thinks the most important quality to possess is _____ .
   Ⓐ wisdom   Ⓑ diligence
   Ⓒ merit   Ⓓ team work

18. What does Mr. Boon find in his food?

(A) a banana leaf

(B) a single grain of rice

(C) the promised reward

(D) fricassee of dragon

19. In the story "Virtue Goes to Town," why does it take twenty cooks to feed a single worker?

_____

_____

_____

_____

_____

20. How is the lesson that Virtue learns like the one that the men in "Who Is Best?" learn?

_____

_____

_____

_____

_____

_____

© Harcourt

Iditarod Dream

Directions: For items 1–18, fill in the circle in front of the correct answer. For items 19–20, write the answer.

Vocabulary

1. We visited campaign _____, where all the buttons, banners, and gift items are stored.

- Ⓐ handlers
- Ⓒ tangle
- Ⓑ headquarters
- Ⓓ homeland

2. When the skaters drew numbers for their _____ in the contest, Kate's number had her skating last.

- Ⓐ headquarters
- Ⓒ pace
- Ⓑ handlers
- Ⓓ positions

3. At the circus, animal _____ must have a lot of knowledge about caring for animals.

- Ⓐ positions
- Ⓒ tangle
- Ⓑ headquarters
- Ⓓ handlers

4. My fishing line got wrapped up with my friend's line, making one huge _____ .

- Ⓐ destiny
- Ⓒ tangle
- Ⓑ pace
- Ⓓ comment

5. The two joggers moved along the path at a comfortable _____ .

- Ⓐ pace
- Ⓒ positions
- Ⓑ tangle
- Ⓓ destiny

Comprehension

6. How many dog teams are entered in the Jr. Iditarod race?

- Ⓐ 1 dog team
- Ⓒ 3 dog teams
- Ⓑ 15 dog teams
- Ⓓ 16 dog teams

Practice Book
Distant Voyages

7. The number one position in the Jr. Iditarod race is _____ .

   Ⓐ dedicated to a supporter of that year's race

   Ⓑ given to the winner of last year's race

   Ⓒ picked by Andy Willis, this year's favorite

   Ⓓ reserved for the winner of the Trail-Sled-Dog Race

8. Why is Dusty glad the temperature is zero degrees?

   Ⓐ Dusty likes to race in cold weather.

   Ⓑ The dogs will not be too cold.

   Ⓒ The frozen river will not melt.

   Ⓓ The dogs will not get overheated.

9. Why does the starting place of this race concern Dusty?

   Ⓐ The lake is not solidly frozen.

   Ⓑ There are many snowmobiles and obstacles to look out for.

   Ⓒ The lake is covered with snow and can't be seen easily.

   Ⓓ The lake is slippery, and he is afraid he might lose control of the team.

10. According to the selection, what must each racer carry on the sled?

   Ⓐ fuel to make a fire

   Ⓑ blankets

   Ⓒ two pounds of food for each dog

   Ⓓ an emergency first-aid kit

11. Why is a tangle a musher's second-worst nightmare?

   Ⓐ Dogs can injure or strangle themselves.

   Ⓑ A tangle causes the musher to lose time.

   Ⓒ The dogs may fight with one another.

   Ⓓ The dogs get frightened and cannot be controlled.

12. Why did Dusty lose the previous year's race?

   Ⓐ He let his dogs get tangled.

   Ⓑ He rested the dogs too long at Flathorn Lake.

   Ⓒ He took the wrong trail at Flathorn Lake.

   Ⓓ He stayed too long at Yentna Station.

13. Why does Dusty replace Annie as lead dog?

Ⓐ She is too inexperienced.

Ⓑ The near accident with the snowmobile has made her nervous.

Ⓒ Jazz wants to be in the lead with QT.

Ⓓ She seems very tired.

14. Why does Dusty leave Yentna at three-thirty in the morning?

Ⓐ His team has rested for the necessary ten hours.

Ⓑ A big snowstorm is blowing in.

Ⓒ He likes to race in the dark.

Ⓓ Both he and the dogs are rested.

15. Why does Dusty help build a fire at Yentna?

Ⓐ Dusty is not tired.

Ⓑ Dusty needs to warm himself.

Ⓒ People in the wilderness help one another.

Ⓓ The dogs need to warm up by the fire.

16. What rumor is started about Dusty?

Ⓐ that he did not stay at Yentna for ten hours

Ⓑ that he did not follow the whole racecourse

Ⓒ that he did not push his dogs hard enough

Ⓓ that he abused his dogs

17. This selection is a retelling of how Dusty _____ .

Ⓐ lost the previous year's Jr. Iditarod race

Ⓑ trains his dog team

Ⓒ loses the Jr. Iditarod race

Ⓓ runs and wins the Jr. Iditarod race

18. This nonfiction selection is most like _____ .

Ⓐ a folktale

Ⓑ a personal diary

Ⓒ an informational article

Ⓓ an interview

19. Why does Dusty have to lift a dog's front legs off the ground when he walks it from the truck?

_____

_____

_____

_____

_____

_____

_____

_____

_____

_____

20. How does everyone know that Dusty has not hurt his dogs?

_____

_____

_____

_____

_____

_____

_____

_____

_____

_____

Practice Book
Distant Voyages

Woodsong

Directions: For items 1–18, fill in the circle in front of the correct answer. For items 19–20, write the answer.

Vocabulary

1. When my brother grew up, he _____ my father so much that people often got them mixed up.
   - Ⓐ resembled
   - Ⓑ plodded
   - Ⓒ retired
   - Ⓓ pointedly

2. I had trouble lifting the box because of its weight and its _____ .
   - Ⓐ snort
   - Ⓑ disengage
   - Ⓒ bulk
   - Ⓓ kindness

3. After the horse got too old to pull a plow, we _____ him and let him graze in the field.
   - Ⓐ resembled
   - Ⓑ retired
   - Ⓒ pointedly
   - Ⓓ disengage

4. The rancher put a _____ on the horse so that it could pull the wagon.
   - Ⓐ retired
   - Ⓑ harness
   - Ⓒ snort
   - Ⓓ bulk

5. I tried to _____ the latch in the barn door to get the door to open.
   - Ⓐ pointedly
   - Ⓑ resembled
   - Ⓒ retired
   - Ⓓ disengage

6. My friend _____ threw the ball toward me, knowing that I would be able to catch it.
   - Ⓐ resembled
   - Ⓑ harness
   - Ⓒ retired
   - Ⓓ pointedly

7. Horses make loud noises when they _____ .
   - Ⓐ harness
   - Ⓑ bulk
   - Ⓒ snort
   - Ⓓ bark

Practice Book
Distant Voyages

Comprehension

8. Why did the author write about Storm?
   - (A) because he and Storm traveled together so much
   - (B) because he wanted to show that dogs can teach mushers a lot
   - (C) because he wanted to show how a bad dog affects the other dogs
   - (D) because Storm was his last dog

9. How did the author feel about Storm?
   - (A) Storm was funny-looking because of his bear's ears.
   - (B) The author liked all dogs and felt it was possible to learn from them.
   - (C) The author learned about life from Storm and greatly respected him.
   - (D) The author was annoyed that Storm played tricks on him.

10. When Storm was too old to pull, he _____ .
   - (A) trained puppies to pull
   - (B) played tricks on his owner
   - (C) fought with Fonzie
   - (D) ran beside the sled

11. When Storm was bored by pulling a sled, he _____ .
   - (A) sat down and refused to pull
   - (B) tickled the ear of the dog next to him
   - (C) hid his booties
   - (D) bit the harness of the dog next to him

12. How did the author feel about the tricks that Storm played?
   - (A) angry
   - (B) excited
   - (C) amused
   - (D) disappointed

13. The author compared Storm's eyes to _____ .
   - (A) those of George Burns
   - (B) an enormous stove
   - (C) a scale
   - (D) a heavy weight

© Harcourt

14. When Storm was running a great distance, he would _____ .

Ⓐ tire easily

Ⓑ always want to be the lead dog

Ⓒ growl at the sled

Ⓓ break a branch from a tree and carry it

15. If Storm was not pleased with what the author was doing with the dogs, Storm would _____ .

Ⓐ bark loudly

Ⓑ refuse to take his stick

Ⓒ chew on his stick

Ⓓ bite the author's hand

16. Why was the trip to pick up the stove tiring for the dogs?

Ⓐ because it was all uphill

Ⓑ because the stove was very far away

Ⓒ because it followed the railroad tracks

Ⓓ because they were the first to go through the new snow

17. How many miles did Storm and the author run together?

Ⓐ thousands of miles

Ⓑ millions of miles

Ⓒ many hundreds of miles

Ⓓ a few hundred miles

18. The author felt that he and Storm were a team because _____ .

Ⓐ Storm followed him everywhere he went

Ⓑ Storm played tricks on him

Ⓒ Storm was obedient

Ⓓ Storm knew the author better than his family did

Practice Book
Distant Voyages

19. Name three things that Storm hid from his owner.

_____

_____

_____

_____

_____

_____

_____

20. How are "Iditarod Dream" and "Woodsong" alike? How are the two selections different?

_____

_____

_____

_____

_____

_____

_____

_____

_____

_____

_____

© Harcourt

Directions: For items 1–18, fill in the circle in front of the correct answer.
For items 19–20, write the answer.

Vocabulary

1. The peacock with all its beautiful feathers appears _____ than other birds when it struts about.
   - Ⓐ pitched
   - Ⓒ vainer
   - Ⓑ forlorn
   - Ⓓ overcome

2. The little lost puppy looked _____ as it wandered aimlessly in the park.
   - Ⓐ pointedly
   - Ⓒ pitched
   - Ⓑ forlorn
   - Ⓓ abalone

3. The bear prepared its _____ for the long winter ahead.
   - Ⓐ vainer
   - Ⓒ lair
   - Ⓑ overcome
   - Ⓓ gorged

4. The _____ , a sea animal, lives in its shell.
   - Ⓐ abalone
   - Ⓒ resembled
   - Ⓑ lair
   - Ⓓ forlorn

5. Everyone was so hungry after the long swim, they _____ themselves.
   - Ⓐ vainer
   - Ⓒ gorged
   - Ⓑ overcome
   - Ⓓ pitched

6. Throughout the hurricane, the ship _____ about on the waves.
   - Ⓐ pitched
   - Ⓒ gorged
   - Ⓑ overcome
   - Ⓓ forlorn

7. I was _____ with fear that the ship would sink during the violent storm.
   - Ⓐ vainer
   - Ⓒ abalone
   - Ⓑ forlorn
   - Ⓓ overcome

Comprehension

8. Why is Nanko asking everyone to hurry?

   Ⓐ The ship is preparing to leave.

   Ⓑ It is raining hard.

   Ⓒ He is angry that the women are so slow.

   Ⓓ He can see a bad windstorm in the distance.

9. Why does Ulape have more boxes of earrings than her sister?

   Ⓐ Ulape's ears are bigger.

   Ⓑ Ulape is older.

   Ⓒ Ulape likes earrings better.

   Ⓓ Ulape is more interested in how she looks.

10. What does it mean when there is a blue clay mark across a woman's nose and cheekbones?

   Ⓐ She is married.

   Ⓑ She is single.

   Ⓒ She is engaged.

   Ⓓ Someone in her family has died.

11. Ramo forgets to take his _____ .

   Ⓐ clothes   Ⓑ knife

   Ⓒ fishing rod   Ⓓ fishing spear

12. Who is telling the story?

   Ⓐ Ramo   Ⓑ Chief Matasaip

   Ⓒ Nanko   Ⓓ Ramo's sister

13. Why does the storyteller jump overboard when the ship heads east?

   Ⓐ She wants to go for a swim.

   Ⓑ She is escaping from Nanko.

   Ⓒ She realizes the ship is not going back for Ramo.

   Ⓓ She wants to gather kelp along the shore.

© Harcourt

14. Why does the storyteller hug Ramo instead of punishing him?

(A) because she is so angry with him and she is afraid she will hurt him

(B) because she decides she will punish him later

(C) because she is so glad to see him that she forgets she is angry with him

(D) because she is happy that she has reached land safely

15. Why did Ramo and the storyteller have trouble finding food in the village?

(A) The villagers took all the food with them when they left.

(B) A pack of dogs entered the village and ate everything.

(C) The storyteller dropped all her cooking utensils when she swam ashore.

(D) They did not know where the food was stored.

16. How does Ramo make up for the trouble he has caused the storyteller?

(A) He fishes and helps weave a basket.

(B) He makes new bowls for her.

(C) He protects her from the wild dogs.

(D) He builds a new house for them.

17. The wild dogs do not attack Ramo and his sister at night because they _____ .

(A) give them food to eat

(B) keep the fire burning all night

(C) chase them away

(D) play with the dogs

18. Why does the storyteller say that the ship might come back in a long time?

(A) She thinks the ship will return for them.

(B) Another storm is coming.

(C) The hunters have now left the island.

(D) She doesn't want Ramo to know they are there alone.

19. How does Ramo feel about the storyteller swimming back to join him? Explain.

_____

_____

_____

_____

_____

_____

_____

_____

20. How does Ramo intend to get larger amounts of fish for food?

_____

_____

_____

_____

_____

_____

_____

_____

© Harcourt

Practice Book
Distant Voyages

Everglades

Directions: For items 1–18, fill in the circle in front of the correct answer. For items 19–20, write the answer.

Vocabulary

1. As the wolf approached the clearing, the other animals _____ off to safety.
   - (A) pondered
   - (B) multitude
   - (C) scurried
   - (D) peninsula

2. A _____ of people will attend the playoff games each year.
   - (A) peninsula
   - (B) multitude
   - (C) pondered
   - (D) scurried

3. Scientists measure the age of a galaxy in _____ .
   - (A) plenitude
   - (B) eons
   - (C) scurried
   - (D) pondered

4. We get lots of ocean breezes at the cottage because it is located on a _____ that juts into the ocean.
   - (A) peninsula
   - (B) plenitude
   - (C) multitude
   - (D) pondered

5. A _____ of orange blossoms will bloom, filling the grove with a wonderful scent.
   - (A) peninsula
   - (B) plenitude
   - (C) pondered
   - (D) scurried

6. Students _____ the ideas presented in the video on life in outer space.
   - (A) scurried
   - (B) multitude
   - (C) pondered
   - (D) entrusted

Practice Book
Distant Voyages

Comprehension

7. _____ is rock formed on the bottom of the sea by seashells.

Ⓐ Sandstone   Ⓑ Quicksilver

Ⓒ Saw grass   Ⓓ Limestone

8. Alligators can walk unhurt among the spears of saw grass because they _____ .

Ⓐ have very tough skin

Ⓑ have large teeth to chew the saw grass

Ⓒ crawl under the saw grass spears

Ⓓ eat the spikes of the spears

9. Who were the first people to come to the Everglades?

Ⓐ Spanish conquistadors

Ⓑ Seminole Indians

Ⓒ Creek Indians

Ⓓ Calusas

10. Who were the next people to move to the Everglades?

Ⓐ Spanish conquistadors   Ⓑ Seminole Indians

Ⓒ Creek Indians   Ⓓ Calusas

11. In this selection, the author describes the Everglades as a "living kaleidoscope of color and beauty" because _____ .

Ⓐ many kinds of trees, flowers, and animals live there

Ⓑ the pieces of glass in the kaleidoscope change color constantly

Ⓒ orchids grow along the sides of the trees

Ⓓ the birds are as colorful as the flowers

12. According to the selection, egrets almost became extinct because _____ .

Ⓐ they were killed by other animals for food

Ⓑ Indians used their feathers for headdresses

Ⓒ hunters sold their feathers to decorate women's hats

Ⓓ the winters became too cold for them

13. The state of Florida is a _____ .
- Ⓐ triangle
- Ⓑ long rectangle
- Ⓒ grassy island
- Ⓓ peninsula

14. When Lake Okeechobee flooded, the spill _____ .
- Ⓐ flooded Miami
- Ⓑ became a river
- Ⓒ formed waterfalls
- Ⓓ filled holes with limestone

15. The Spanish conquistadors left Florida because _____ .
- Ⓐ it was too hot for them
- Ⓑ alligators attacked them
- Ⓒ the land was too jungle-like
- Ⓓ Creek Indians drove them out

16. Which group of early visitors still has some people living in the Everglades?
- Ⓐ Spanish conquistadors
- Ⓑ Seminole Indians
- Ⓒ Creek Indians
- Ⓓ Calusas

17. The beginning of this selection describes the Everglades _____ .
- Ⓐ as they are today
- Ⓑ during the Age of Seashells
- Ⓒ during the Age of Exploration
- Ⓓ in the early 20th century

18. At the end of the selection, the children want to return home quickly so they can _____ .
- Ⓐ have dinner
- Ⓑ watch television
- Ⓒ grow up and save the Everglades
- Ⓓ grow up and build large cities

19. What is the sad story the children heard?

_____

_____

_____

_____

_____

_____

_____

_____

_____

20. What is the happy story the children heard?

_____

_____

_____

_____

_____

_____

_____

_____

_____

© Harcourt

Practice Book
Distant Voyages

Summer of Fire

Directions: For items 1–18, fill in the circle in front of the correct answer. For items 19–20, write the answer.

Vocabulary

1. The campers gathered dry twigs and leaves to use as _____ to start a campfire.
- Ⓐ canopy
- Ⓑ tinder
- Ⓒ policy
- Ⓓ dwindled

2. Our supplies _____ down until we had only bread and water to eat and drink.
- Ⓐ dwindled
- Ⓑ veered
- Ⓒ policy
- Ⓓ geyser

3. The fire had gone out, but glowing _____ remained in the ashes.
- Ⓐ policy
- Ⓑ dwindled
- Ⓒ canopy
- Ⓓ embers

4. Chewing gum in school is against our school _____ .
- Ⓐ geyser
- Ⓑ policy
- Ⓒ embers
- Ⓓ canopy

5. The tourists were amazed by the hot water and steam shooting up from the _____ .
- Ⓐ geyser
- Ⓑ canopy
- Ⓒ dwindled
- Ⓓ policy

6. We accidentally _____ off course for a few miles, but now we are headed in the right direction.
- Ⓐ tinder
- Ⓑ dwindled
- Ⓒ embers
- Ⓓ veered

7. The tall trees and leaves form a _____ in the forest.
- Ⓐ geyser
- Ⓑ canopy
- Ⓒ policy
- Ⓓ tinder

Practice Book
Distant Voyages

Comprehension

8. What are the summers in Yellowstone Park often like?

(A) short and dry 　　(B) short and rainy

(C) long and dry 　　(D) long and rainy

9. What was the usual policy in Yellowstone Park regarding wildfires?

(A) to only put out fires that were in heavily populated areas and caused by humans

(B) to put out wildfires only

(C) to let wildfires burn unless they were dangerous to lives or property

(D) to put out all fires

10. The number of lightning strikes in Yellowstone in 1988 was _____ .

(A) half the usual number

(B) about the usual number

(C) twice the usual number

(D) three times the usual number

11. The cold fronts made it difficult to fight the fires because _____ .

(A) winds bring oxygen to the fires

(B) cold fronts bring hurricanes

(C) rain increases the amount of smoke

(D) they make the fire fighters cold

12. "Sheets of flame leaped forward." In this selection, *sheets* means _____ .

(A) large pieces of paper

(B) large continuous surfaces or layers

(C) pieces of cloth used on beds

(D) flat, metal baking pans

13. How many acres of forests burned on Black Saturday?

(A) less than 150 acres

(B) less than 1,500 acres

(C) more than 150,000 acres

(D) more than 1 million acres

Practice Book
Distant Voyages

14. What caused most of the Yellowstone fires during the summer of 1988?

Ⓐ weather

Ⓑ human carelessness

Ⓒ park policy

Ⓓ poor fire-fighting equipment

15. Before fire fighters at Old Faithful saw the flames of the North Fork fire, they _____ .

Ⓐ saw snowflakes

Ⓑ heard the fire

Ⓒ felt the temperature fall

Ⓓ saw exploding boulders

16. The buildings around Old Faithful did not burn because _____ .

Ⓐ helicopters dropped chemicals on them

Ⓑ fire fighters wet them down with water

Ⓒ the wind turned the fire away from the area

Ⓓ the rains finally came

17. Which of the following is true about Yellowstone?

Ⓐ Most of Yellowstone was destroyed by fire.

Ⓑ Fire destroyed Yellowstone's geysers, steam vents, and hot springs.

Ⓒ Some of the buildings in Yellowstone burned.

Ⓓ Yellowstone needs fire to renew its plant growth.

18. How much of Yellowstone Park was destroyed by fire?

Ⓐ one-third

Ⓑ one-fifth

Ⓒ one-half

Ⓓ two-thirds

19. When did the fires finally stop burning in Yellowstone?

_____

_____

_____

_____

_____

_____

_____

_____

_____

20. Explain why the author thinks Yellowstone needs fire as much as it needs sun and rain.

_____

_____

_____

_____

_____

_____

_____

_____

_____

© Harcourt

Oceans

Directions: For items 1–18, fill in the circle in front of the correct answer. For items 19–20, write the answer.

Vocabulary

1. Energy is _____ by water passing over the paddles of the mill.
   - Ⓐ generated
   - Ⓑ shallow
   - Ⓒ bulge
   - Ⓓ gravitational

2. We could see minnows swimming in the _____ waters, close to the bank of the river.
   - Ⓐ energy
   - Ⓑ shallow
   - Ⓒ generated
   - Ⓓ burning

3. The large ship was not able to sail into the _____ because the water was too shallow.
   - Ⓐ generated
   - Ⓑ energy
   - Ⓒ geyser
   - Ⓓ inlet

4. Ocean tides are caused by the _____ pull of the sun and the moon.
   - Ⓐ energy
   - Ⓑ bulge
   - Ⓒ gravitational
   - Ⓓ generated

5. Mother had to get a new tire for her car because of the _____ on the side of the tire.
   - Ⓐ inlet
   - Ⓑ bulge
   - Ⓒ shallow
   - Ⓓ burrow

6. Food supplies our bodies with _____ so we can move and grow.
   - Ⓐ energy
   - Ⓑ shallow
   - Ⓒ bulge
   - Ⓓ dignity

Comprehension

7. This selection is most like _____ .
   - Ⓐ a biography
   - Ⓑ science fiction
   - Ⓒ an anecdote
   - Ⓓ a science textbook

Practice Book
Distant Voyages

8. Most places along the coast have two high and two low tides daily because _____ .

   Ⓐ the sun and the moon pull at right angles

   Ⓑ of double tidal bulges

   Ⓒ spring and neap tides disappear from sight

   Ⓓ the moon's pull is stronger than the sun's

9. Earth is different from the other planets in that _____ .

   Ⓐ it has no water at all, and the other planets do

   Ⓑ it is the only planet with liquid water on its surface

   Ⓒ it is shaped differently than the other planets

   Ⓓ it has no human life on it, and the others do

10. Tides are caused by the gravitational pull of the _____ .

   Ⓐ oceans and the land

   Ⓑ planets and the stars

   Ⓒ islands and the rocks

   Ⓓ sun and the moon

11. How are spring tides different from neap tides?

   Ⓐ Spring tides are smaller than neap tides.

   Ⓑ They are not different in any way.

   Ⓒ Spring tides are bigger tides than neap tides.

   Ⓓ Only spring tides are caused by the sun.

12. A tsunami is very dangerous because _____ .

   Ⓐ it is so slow moving

   Ⓑ it has high winds

   Ⓒ it is only a few feet high

   Ⓓ it can strike with huge force

13. According to the selection, the *fetch* of a wave is _____ .

   Ⓐ the length of the wave

   Ⓑ the height of the wave

   Ⓒ the distance over which the wave travels

   Ⓓ the speed of the wind over a wave

© Harcourt

14. If you were in the middle of the ocean where the wind is blowing, you would see _____ .

Ⓐ all different kinds of waves

Ⓑ no waves at all

Ⓒ huge waves only

Ⓓ waves moving all in the same direction

15. The author uses the example of the bobbing stick on the ocean to show that _____ .

Ⓐ sticks float

Ⓑ the wave moves everything in its path

Ⓒ water does not move along with a wave

Ⓓ waves can be powerful

16. The height of the largest wave on record is as tall as _____ .

Ⓐ a two-story house

Ⓑ a ten-story building

Ⓒ an NBA basketball player

Ⓓ a skyscraper

17. In this selection, the phrase *the wave begins to feel the bottom* means that _____ .

Ⓐ it is in the deepest part of the ocean

Ⓑ it is moving as fast as it can

Ⓒ the wave keeps hitting the bottom of the ocean

Ⓓ the wave travels more slowly and changes shape

18. A breaker happens only after the wave slows down and _____ .

Ⓐ falls into the trough of the wave in front of it

Ⓑ then picks up speed

Ⓒ gets smaller in size on a sandy beach

Ⓓ is out in deep water

Practice Book
Distant Voyages

19. Ships should not sail during severe storms because

_____

_____

_____

_____

_____

_____

_____

20. What proof is there that the sea can change land formations?

_____

_____

_____

_____

_____

_____

_____

_____

© Harcourt

Practice Book
Distant Voyages

Seeing Earth from Space

Directions: For items 1–18, fill in the circle in front of the correct answer. For items 19–20, write the answer.

Vocabulary

1. We decided to take our time and _____ through the woods, enjoying the sights along the path.

Ⓐ meander   Ⓑ lagoon

Ⓒ reef   Ⓓ mentor

2. Swimmers splashed in the shallow _____, encircled by the coral island.

Ⓐ barren   Ⓑ meander

Ⓒ lagoon   Ⓓ office

3. On vacation we swam in the lagoon and jogged around the entire _____.

Ⓐ sensor   Ⓑ atoll

Ⓒ barren   Ⓓ lair

4. The garage door opener has _____ to stop the door from crushing small animals.

Ⓐ lagoon   Ⓑ barren

Ⓒ reefs   Ⓓ sensors

5. It has been so long since the _____ desert has had any rain that even the cactus may not survive.

Ⓐ meander   Ⓑ barren

Ⓒ bushy   Ⓓ atoll

6. When we went snorkeling, we explored a beautiful coral _____.

Ⓐ reef   Ⓑ barren

Ⓒ sensor   Ⓓ hoof

© Harcourt

Comprehension

7. The *Apollo 8* astronauts were the first to _____ .

- (A) go on a sight-seeing trip
- (B) see the full face of the Earth
- (C) orbit the sun
- (D) see Earth as a planet

8. How fast is Earth traveling around the sun?

- (A) 67,000 miles a light year
- (B) 6,700 miles an hour
- (C) 67,000 miles an hour
- (D) 6,700 miles a minute

9. How are the pictures of Earth taken from satellites different from those taken by astronauts orbiting above the Earth?

- (A) The pictures show the full length of rivers.
- (B) The pictures show things that can't be seen by human beings.
- (C) The pictures show details of Earth, but not the whole Earth.
- (D) Satellites carry sensors and radar for taking pictures.

10. What causes the golden haze over the Indian Ocean?

- (A) sunlight
- (B) clouds
- (C) Typhoon Pat
- (D) air pollution

11. How are most islands formed?

- (A) by earthquakes
- (B) by volcanoes under the ocean
- (C) by volcanoes on land
- (D) by giant storms

12. Coral is a kind of _____ .

- (A) rock
- (B) plant
- (C) animal
- (D) sand

© Harcourt

Practice Book
Distant Voyages

13. The Himalayas were formed when _____ .

(A) the ocean floor was pushed up

(B) huge pieces of the earth's crust were pressed together

(C) huge lava flows were built up

(D) two islands collided

14. The astronauts found that stars are brighter when they are seen from the moon because _____ .

(A) the moon has no atmosphere to dim the light

(B) Earth is farther away from the stars

(C) Earth is whirling at 67,000 miles an hour

(D) Earth is closer to the sun than the moon is

15. What excited the Apollo astronauts most about the sight of Earth?

(A) It was home.

(B) It was colorful.

(C) It was in a black sea of space.

(D) There was life on Earth.

16. "From space they see that the atmosphere is only a thin shell surrounding the earth." In this selection, *atmosphere* means _____ .

(A) darkness   (B) water

(C) light   (D) air

17. Which sentence best describes how people who have traveled in space feel about the earth?

(A) The earth is large and sturdy.

(B) The earth's atmosphere is boundless.

(C) The earth is one world for all people.

(D) The earth is divided into many countries.

18. What is the author's main purpose for writing this selection?

(A) to encourage the reader to become an astronaut

(B) to help the reader appreciate the earth

(C) to explain the solar system

(D) to give information about islands

19. What is the atmosphere like for people on Earth? What is the atmosphere like when it is seen from space?

_____

_____

_____

_____

_____

_____

_____

_____

_____

_____

20. Name three parts of the earth that need protection.

_____

_____

_____

_____

_____

_____

_____

_____

_____

_____

_____

Practice Book
Distant Voyages

The Case of the Flying-Saucer People

Directions: For items 1–18, fill in the circle in front of the correct answer. For items 19–20, write the answer.

Vocabulary

1. My friend completed a Spanish _____ of one of my favorite stories.
   - Ⓐ advanced
   - Ⓑ piercing
   - Ⓒ translation
   - Ⓓ decoration

2. The new announcer has black, _____ eyes that seem to look right through you when he speaks.
   - Ⓐ piercing
   - Ⓑ features
   - Ⓒ publicity
   - Ⓓ measuring

3. The author appeared on television and talked about her new book because she wanted _____ .
   - Ⓐ translation
   - Ⓑ publicity
   - Ⓒ feature
   - Ⓓ commotion

4. Next year, I will take an _____ Spanish class.
   - Ⓐ atoll
   - Ⓑ advanced
   - Ⓒ energy
   - Ⓓ embers

5. Which of the _____ in the new house do you like best?
   - Ⓐ features
   - Ⓑ piercing
   - Ⓒ advanced
   - Ⓓ weird

Comprehension

6. Einstein enjoys using words out of order, but others find this habit to be _____ .
   - Ⓐ funny
   - Ⓑ confusing
   - Ⓒ annoying
   - Ⓓ sincere

7. *Einstein* is not his real name; _____ .

Ⓐ his mother calls him Adam

Ⓑ his brother is called Dennis

Ⓒ other people like his name

Ⓓ it's his brother's name

8. Why does Mrs. Anderson invite Mr. Janus to dinner?

Ⓐ She wants her family to meet him.

Ⓑ She wants to buy his translation machine.

Ⓒ He is new in town and doesn't know anyone.

Ⓓ She is interviewing him and wants Einstein to check his story.

9. In the selection, what evidence leads you to think Mrs. Anderson may doubt Mr. Janus's story?

Ⓐ Mr. Janus sounds very sincere.

Ⓑ She doesn't believe in flying saucers.

Ⓒ She wants Einstein's opinion about Mr. Janus's adventure.

Ⓓ She has been to the base station but did not meet Mr. Janus.

10. According to Mr. Janus, it was not difficult to climb the hill on the moon because _____ .

Ⓐ the hill was small

Ⓑ of the moon's high gravity

Ⓒ of the moon's low gravity

Ⓓ there was a comfortable breeze

11. One way the moon is different from earth is that the moon _____ .

Ⓐ is hotter than earth

Ⓑ has no atmosphere

Ⓒ is colder than earth

Ⓓ has lots of dust and rocks

© Harcourt

12. Why are the saucer people destroying their base?

(A) The saucer people are planning to enlarge the base.

(B) The saucer people think Earth people are too advanced to move there.

(C) Earth people are not advanced enough to belong to the Galaxy Federation of Intelligent Beings.

(D) Earth people already belong to the Galaxy Federation of Intelligent Beings.

13. In this selection, the word *whopper* refers to a big, fat _____ .

(A) hamburger

(B) fiction book

(C) lie

(D) scientific error

14. In order for sound waves to travel and be heard, there must be _____ .

(A) land

(B) sunlight

(C) water

(D) air

15. According to this selection, at one hundred degrees Celsius, water will _____ .

(A) begin to boil

(B) be a little warm

(C) be at room temperature

(D) turn to ice

16. This selection mostly takes place _____ .

(A) in a modern-day home

(B) at the newspaper office

(C) on the moon

(D) in the flying saucer

Practice Book
Distant Voyages

17. This selection is a mystery because _____ .
   Ⓐ it gives instructions for making something
   Ⓑ it tells a true story about someone's life
   Ⓒ the action focuses on solving a mystery
   Ⓓ it solves a word puzzle

18. What does Einstein think he will be in two years?
   Ⓐ a very important detective
   Ⓑ fourteen
   Ⓒ an interviewer
   Ⓓ one of the flying-saucer people

19. How does Mr. Janus describe the saucer people?

_____

_____

_____

_____

_____

_____

20. What do the saucer people do that leads you to believe they had not planned to harm Mr. Janus?

_____

_____

_____

_____

_____

Hattie's Birthday Box

Directions: For items 1–18, fill in the circle in front of the correct answer. For items 19–20, write the answer.

Vocabulary

1. Thinking fast, Brianna _____ a story to explain how the window got broken.
   - Ⓐ brooded
   - Ⓑ concocted
   - Ⓒ perched
   - Ⓓ firmed

2. From her _____ high on the cliff, Tina could see out over the ocean for miles.
   - Ⓐ despair
   - Ⓑ rations
   - Ⓒ perch
   - Ⓓ creature

3. Lance _____ all day about the possibility that his team might lose the game.
   - Ⓐ rationed
   - Ⓑ concocted
   - Ⓒ brooded
   - Ⓓ invested

4. On our camping trip, we had enough _____ for only a week.
   - Ⓐ rations
   - Ⓑ perch
   - Ⓒ homestead
   - Ⓓ shadows

5. The facts in the case are _____ and prove that the defendant is innocent.
   - Ⓐ despair
   - Ⓑ homestead
   - Ⓒ brooded
   - Ⓓ undeniable

6. Long ago many families moved west to _____ instead of staying in the crowded cities.
   - Ⓐ concocted
   - Ⓑ perch
   - Ⓒ homestead
   - Ⓓ settlement

7. Nick was overcome with a feeling of _____ because he thought he would never finish the project.
   - Ⓐ despair
   - Ⓑ brooded
   - Ⓒ homestead
   - Ⓓ repair

Practice Book
Distant Voyages

Comprehension

8. Why is the whole family gathering?

   (A) to wait for Aunt Hattie's visit

   (B) to visit the nursing home

   (C) to celebrate Grandaddy McClintic's 100th birthday

   (D) to see how many relatives the McClintic family has

9. Relatives can come from near and far to the event for all the following reasons **except** _____ .

   (A) there is no more rationing

   (B) the war is over

   (C) almost everyone is home from the war

   (D) the nursing home is in a central location

10. All the following show that Grandaddy is nervous **except** _____ .

   (A) he sits in his chair by the window

   (B) he rubs his hands together

   (C) he repeatedly asks Anna who is coming

   (D) he taps his slippered feet

11. Why did Grandaddy stew and brood the night before Hattie left for Nebraska?

   (A) Hattie was just sixteen years old.

   (B) Hattie had just gotten married.

   (C) There was a combination going-away and birthday party for Hattie.

   (D) He had nothing to put into the box he made for her.

12. Why does Grandaddy make up his tale about the box?

   (A) to keep from telling Hattie that he has no real gift for her

   (B) to show how good he is at woodworking

   (C) to make it all right that he made the gift

   (D) to prove what a good storyteller he is

13. Why is Grandaddy nervous about Hattie's visit?
- (A) because he has turned 100 years old
- (B) because he thinks she is mad at him
- (C) because his whole family is there
- (D) because he loves his sister

14. Why doesn't Grandaddy ever buy something for Hattie's birthday box?
- (A) He never has the money.
- (B) Hattie is far away in Nebraska.
- (C) Hattie doesn't need any more presents.
- (D) Time goes on, and he never gets around to it.

15. Hattie says, "Oh, Spencer, Spencer, there's been too much time and space." What does she mean?
- (A) Seventy-four years is a long time.
- (B) Nebraska is very far away from here.
- (C) She is asking her brother why he never came to visit.
- (D) They have been away from each other far too long.

16. What lesson did Hattie learn the first winter when she and Otto ran out of food?
- (A) to let people help their neighbors
- (B) to let Otto have his pride
- (C) to keep extra food in the cupboard
- (D) to always be proud

17. Why does Hattie finally open the box?
- (A) Her children are starving.
- (B) She needs something to sell.
- (C) She wants to honor Spencer by wearing what's inside.
- (D) Her husband needs a wagon for traveling to Nebraska.

18. Which word best describes Hattie?
- (A) hopeful
- (B) angry
- (C) proud
- (D) helpful

19. In Hattie's box, the granddaughter smells "a young farmer's stubbornness, a pioneer mother's sorrow, and a wondrous wild and lasting hope." Name one event in Hattie's life that goes with each.

_____

_____

_____

_____

_____

_____

_____

_____

_____

20. Why is the empty box the best gift Hattie ever received?

_____

_____

_____

_____

_____

_____

_____

_____

_____

_____

Practice Book
Distant Voyages

William Shakespeare & the Globe

Directions: For items 1–18, fill in the circle in front of the correct answer. For items 19–20, write the answer.

Vocabulary

1. Because the bridge was closed and cars could not get across the river, the traffic was more _____ than usual.

Ⓐ lavish   Ⓑ congested

Ⓒ patron   Ⓓ assured

2. The carpenter wanted to save the beams in the old barn, so he tried to _____ the barn carefully.

Ⓐ adornment   Ⓑ lavish

Ⓒ dismantle   Ⓓ critical

3. The professional musicians in the audience were _____ of the student's violin solo.

Ⓐ patron   Ⓑ shareholder

Ⓒ congested   Ⓓ critical

4. Over the years, many famous artists have been given support by a generous _____ .

Ⓐ patron   Ⓑ adornment

Ⓒ lavish   Ⓓ please

5. Each _____ paid $1,000 to be part owner in the new business.

Ⓐ adornment   Ⓑ congested

Ⓒ shareholder   Ⓓ handler

6. In plays today, many of the sets and costumes are _____ and very fancy.

Ⓐ dismantle   Ⓑ lavish

Ⓒ adornment   Ⓓ congested

7. The _____ of a crown and the regal robes left no doubt in the audience's mind which actor was the king.

Ⓐ critical   Ⓑ shareholder

Ⓒ patron   Ⓓ adornment

Comprehension

8. Shakespeare, a great storyteller, mainly wrote _____ .

Ⓐ novels

Ⓑ operas

Ⓒ plays

Ⓓ children's stories

9. In this selection, the Globe is a _____ .

Ⓐ playhouse

Ⓑ world atlas

Ⓒ bridge

Ⓓ summer residence

10. James Burbage's sons named their new playhouse the _____ .

Ⓐ Thames

Ⓑ Globe

Ⓒ Stage

Ⓓ Bridge

11. Which English royalty lived at the same time as Shakespeare?

Ⓐ Victoria and James I

Ⓑ Elizabeth I and James I

Ⓒ Henry VIII

Ⓓ Elizabeth II and Prince Charles

12. According to this selection, Shakespeare became prosperous because _____ .

Ⓐ the king and queen liked his plays

Ⓑ the Globe made a lot of money for him

Ⓒ of his writings and being part owner of the Globe

Ⓓ he had several very rich patrons

Practice Book
Distant Voyages

13. The Globe theater was different from other theaters at that time because _____ .

Ⓐ it was built long before the other theaters

Ⓑ only nobility attended the plays

Ⓒ it had richly adorned stages, and special effects

Ⓓ it cost more to see a play at the Globe

14. Theatre in Shakespeare's time was different from theatre today because _____ .

Ⓐ people ate, drank, and talked during the performance

Ⓑ tickets were very expensive

Ⓒ the people fell ill

Ⓓ only the nobility attended the theatre

15. The Earl of Southhampton became Shakespeare's patron because _____ .

Ⓐ the Earl was a young noblemen

Ⓑ Shakespeare dedicated a building to him

Ⓒ Shakespeare dedicated two poems to him

Ⓓ the Earl thought Shakespeare was a wonderful actor

16. In Shakespeare's time, a *groundling* was a person who _____ .

Ⓐ was well off and sat in the Lords' Room

Ⓑ sat on cushions in the Gentlemen's Room

Ⓒ stood out in the yard of the playhouse

Ⓓ collected tickets at the playhouse

17. A new kind of indoor playhouse was designed by _____ .

Ⓐ James I   Ⓑ Ben Jonson

Ⓒ Inigo Jones   Ⓓ The King's Men

18. This selection is most like a _____ .

Ⓐ biography   Ⓑ newspaper article

Ⓒ personal diary   Ⓓ tall tale

Practice Book
Distant Voyages

19. According to the selection, what new form of theatre was being created by Ben Jonson?

_____

_____

_____

_____

_____

_____

_____

_____

_____

20. Explain what Ben Jonson meant when he said that Shakespeare *was not of an age, but for all time!*

_____

_____

_____

_____

_____

_____

_____

_____

Directions: For items 1–18, fill in the circle in front of the correct answer. For items 19–20, write the answer.

Vocabulary

1. I have written a book, and my friend will be _____ it with watercolors.
   - Ⓐ encouraged
   - Ⓑ charcoal
   - Ⓒ pastels
   - Ⓓ illustrating

2. In art class, we have been learning to paint in _____ .
   - Ⓐ pastels
   - Ⓑ encourage
   - Ⓒ illustrating
   - Ⓓ offices

3. In her speech, the astronaut thanked all the people who _____ her to follow her dream.
   - Ⓐ charcoal
   - Ⓑ illustrated
   - Ⓒ encouraged
   - Ⓓ patron

4. This author has written a _____ of adventure books, and I have read them all.
   - Ⓐ pastels
   - Ⓑ series
   - Ⓒ charcoal
   - Ⓓ tangle

5. The art teacher suggested that I use _____ for my black and white illustrations.
   - Ⓐ series
   - Ⓑ charcoal
   - Ⓒ pastels
   - Ⓓ encouraged

Comprehension

6. This selection is most like an _____ .
   - Ⓐ autobiography
   - Ⓑ observation
   - Ⓒ article
   - Ⓓ interview

© Harcourt

Practice Book
Distant Voyages

7. According to William Joyce, King Kong and Stuart are similar because they both are _____ .

   Ⓐ loving characters   Ⓑ very small creatures

   Ⓒ the wrong size   Ⓓ very scary monsters

8. How did television affect William Joyce when he was a child?

   Ⓐ He sometimes got too excited.

   Ⓑ It often bored him.

   Ⓒ It got his imagination going.

   Ⓓ It scared him.

9. "I tried all different mediums—watercolors, oils, pencils, pastels." In this selection, *mediums* refers to _____ .

   Ⓐ the middle of something

   Ⓑ the size of something

   Ⓒ a kind of drawing paper

   Ⓓ various drawing materials

10. What does Joyce mean when he says, "In time I found my own style"?

   Ⓐ that his parents let him take art lessons

   Ⓑ that some of his teachers and librarians encouraged him

   Ⓒ that his art shows his individual personality

   Ⓓ that he wants to study the artwork of famous people

11. How does William Joyce feel about drawing things realistically?

   Ⓐ bored   Ⓑ angry

   Ⓒ excited   Ⓓ nervous

12. How long does it take William Joyce to make a book?

   Ⓐ a couple of years   Ⓑ a couple of months

   Ⓒ varying amounts of time   Ⓓ unknown

13. When Joyce paints with color, why does he only use four colors?

   Ⓐ He likes only four colors.

   Ⓑ They are the only colors he has.

   Ⓒ He can mix any color from those four.

   Ⓓ They are the most watery colors.

14. How do William Joyce's children help him?

  Ⓐ He tries out his stories on them.

  Ⓑ They draw some of his sketches.

  Ⓒ He asks their opinions on his art.

  Ⓓ They give him ideas.

15. For William Joyce, what is the first stage in making a book?

  Ⓐ to draw sketches for the whole book

  Ⓑ to write what all the characters say

  Ⓒ to sketch and write each page, one by one

  Ⓓ to sketch and write several pages as a group

16. What is the first book for which William Joyce is both the author and the illustrator?

  Ⓐ *George Shrinks*

  Ⓑ *Dinosaur Bob*

  Ⓒ *The Leaf Men*

  Ⓓ *Tammy and the Gigantic Fish*

17. What is one thing William Joyce likes to draw?

  Ⓐ fish

  Ⓑ dinosaurs

  Ⓒ teddy bears

  Ⓓ clothes

18. Why did William Joyce write this selection?

  Ⓐ to explain how people should write

  Ⓑ to explain how he works and why

  Ⓒ to advertise his books

  Ⓓ to talk about his family

19. How can you tell if Joyce's ideas often change as he works on a book?

_____

_____

_____

_____

_____

_____

_____

_____

_____

20. At the end of the selection, Joyce says, "I never know where the page will take me, or who I'll meet, or what adventure we may go on." What does he mean?

_____

_____

_____

_____

_____

_____

_____

_____

_____

_____

_____

Practice Book
Distant Voyages

Satchmo's Blues

Directions: For items 1–18, fill in the circle in front of the correct answer.
For items 19–20, write the answer.

Vocabulary

1. Farmers bring fresh fruit and vegetables to town to sell in the _____ market.
   - Ⓐ gravelly
   - Ⓑ produce
   - Ⓒ pawnshop
   - Ⓓ errands

2. Sally's mother asked her to run several _____ for her after school.
   - Ⓐ numerous
   - Ⓑ gravelly
   - Ⓒ produce
   - Ⓓ errands

3. My favorite author has published _____ mystery stories.
   - Ⓐ pawnshop
   - Ⓑ produce
   - Ⓒ numerous
   - Ⓓ solve

4. Since Dad's company does business in several countries, his job requires a lot of _____ travel.
   - Ⓐ international
   - Ⓑ gravelly
   - Ⓒ errands
   - Ⓓ translating

5. There were many beautiful necklaces and watches displayed in the _____ window.
   - Ⓐ produce
   - Ⓑ pawnshop
   - Ⓒ numerous
   - Ⓓ errands

6. Pam's voice sounded _____ because she had a bad cold.
   - Ⓐ international
   - Ⓑ errands
   - Ⓒ gravelly
   - Ⓓ produce

Practice Book
Distant Voyages

Comprehension

7. Why doesn't Louis have a trumpet?

  Ⓐ His family lives on Perdido Street.

  Ⓑ Mama doesn't have any money to buy one.

  Ⓒ Someone steals it.

  Ⓓ His mama doesn't like trumpets.

8. Where does Louis find the horn he wants?

  Ⓐ on the pie man's wooden cart

  Ⓑ in a discount store

  Ⓒ in a music shop

  Ⓓ in a pawnshop window

9. How does Louis feel when he can't play Santiago's horn?

  Ⓐ surprised   Ⓑ relieved

  Ⓒ happy   Ⓓ nervous

10. Why does Louis go back to the shop where the horn is?

  Ⓐ He works there after school.

  Ⓑ He wants to see if the horn is still there.

  Ⓒ His mother tells him to buy the horn.

  Ⓓ The man in the store is friendly.

11. When Louis looks into the mirror and pretends to blow the horn, Mama thinks that he _____ .

  Ⓐ looks perfect   Ⓑ is trying to play high C's

  Ⓒ looks like a fish   Ⓓ should stop pretending

12. Which best describes how Louis felt when he saw a parade?

  Ⓐ angry   Ⓑ surprised

  Ⓒ bored   Ⓓ excited

13. Why does Louis do everything he can to earn five dollars?

  Ⓐ to buy a horn

  Ⓑ to help his mother

  Ⓒ to get a present for his sister

  Ⓓ to buy a train ticket to Chicago

© Harcourt

Practice Book
Distant Voyages

Name _____   **Date** _____

14. Selling the good part of the onions shows that Louis is _____ .
Ⓐ sassy
Ⓑ lazy
Ⓒ clever
Ⓓ thoughtful

15. According to the selection, Mama's jambalaya is made with _____ .
Ⓐ rice and beans
Ⓑ shrimp, lobster, and onions
Ⓒ cajun sausage and corn
Ⓓ shrimp, crabs, and sausage

16. How does Louis's mother help him get the horn?
Ⓐ She finds jobs that he can do for the neighbors.
Ⓑ She gets the shop owner to accept $4 for the horn.
Ⓒ She buys the horn for him.
Ⓓ She gives him a dollar.

17. Louis feels ten feet tall when he leaves the pawnshop because he _____ .
Ⓐ bought his sister a birthday present
Ⓑ pawned his horn
Ⓒ has a horn of his own
Ⓓ could play "Dixie Flyer"

18. Why did the author write this selection?
Ⓐ to teach about the city of New Orleans
Ⓑ to show that young Louis had music inside him
Ⓒ to explain how an interest in music is important in a child's life
Ⓓ to explain what jambalaya is

© Harcourt

Practice Book
Distant Voyages

19. Why is Louis upset when his mother asks him for a quarter to buy food?

_____

_____

_____

_____

_____

_____

_____

_____

20. Do you think Mama really needed Louis's quarter? Tell why or why not.

_____

_____

_____

_____

_____

_____

_____

_____

_____

_____

Practice Book
Distant Voyages

Evelyn Cisneros: Prima Ballerina

Directions: For items 1–18, fill in the circle in front of the correct answer. For items 19–20, write the answer.

Vocabulary

1. Stretching exercises help increase the _____ of your body.
   - Ⓐ flexibility
   - Ⓒ thrived
   - Ⓑ migrant
   - Ⓓ timid

2. Glenn stopped playing basketball after school so that he could _____ more time to training his dog.
   - Ⓐ timid
   - Ⓒ migrant
   - Ⓑ thrived
   - Ⓓ devote

3. Johnny worked as an _____ to a silversmith so that he could learn to work with silver.
   - Ⓐ apprentice
   - Ⓒ education
   - Ⓑ adaptable
   - Ⓓ adornment

4. Our crops _____ in the warm sun and rich soil, so we soon had plenty to eat.
   - Ⓐ devoted
   - Ⓒ frightened
   - Ⓑ thrived
   - Ⓓ concocted

5. My sister is hoping her good grades will help her get a _____ to attend college.
   - Ⓐ flexibility
   - Ⓒ scholarship
   - Ⓑ migrant
   - Ⓓ trainee

6. When the other children teased Mattie about her clothes, she grew more and more _____ .
   - Ⓐ thrived
   - Ⓒ flourished
   - Ⓑ timid
   - Ⓓ flexibility

7. The _____ farm workers move from place to place to work as the various crops become ripe.
   - Ⓐ devote
   - Ⓒ migrant
   - Ⓑ thrived
   - Ⓓ piercing

© Harcourt

Comprehension

8. Who is Evelyn Cisneros?

 Ⓐ a princess   Ⓑ a sleeping beauty

 Ⓒ a musician   Ⓓ a prima ballerina

9. Why was Evelyn shy as a child?

 Ⓐ Children teased her about her looks.

 Ⓑ Her parents were often angry with her.

 Ⓒ Her family moved to a new town.

 Ⓓ Her younger brother was constantly teasing her.

10. What made Evelyn's first ballet classes unpleasant for her?

 Ⓐ She had to do stretching exercises.

 Ⓑ She was awkward.

 Ⓒ She had to practice with other people watching.

 Ⓓ She had to work hard.

11. Evelyn's left foot turned inward slightly. Why did she work to change that?

 Ⓐ so her teacher wouldn't complain about it

 Ⓑ so she would become a better dancer

 Ⓒ so she would stand out from her friends

 Ⓓ so turns and jumps would be easier to do

12. What did Evelyn do to straighten her rounded shoulders?

 Ⓐ exercised to increase her flexibility

 Ⓑ wore a brace on her back

 Ⓒ slept only on her back

 Ⓓ stopped tap dancing

13. "Evelyn taught tap dancing and demonstrated ballet positions for younger students." In this selection, *positions* refers to _____ .

 Ⓐ dances for ballet

 Ⓑ opinions about something

 Ⓒ the space occupied by something

 Ⓓ particular stances in ballet

14. Why did the San Francisco Ballet School offer Evelyn a summer scholarship?

Ⓐ Her teachers recommended her.

Ⓑ She danced at the Pacific Ballet Theatre.

Ⓒ She would teach tap dancing there.

Ⓓ Teachers at the ballet school thought she had talent.

15. Which word best describes how Evelyn felt about her dancing after her experience at the San Francisco Ballet School?

Ⓐ confident   Ⓑ displeased

Ⓒ unsure   Ⓓ discouraged

16. Why did Evelyn accept a scholarship to the summer session of the American Ballet School in New York City?

Ⓐ to get away from dancing

Ⓑ to dance at another top school

Ⓒ to be with a favorite teacher

Ⓓ to become an apprentice

17. Which event made Evelyn famous?

Ⓐ dancing in *A Song for Dead Warriors*

Ⓑ being on television

Ⓒ appearing at the White House

Ⓓ replacing an injured ballerina in New York City

18. This selection is a biography because it _____ .

Ⓐ expresses a newspaper editor's opinion

Ⓑ gives instruction for making something

Ⓒ tells the true story of a person's life

Ⓓ lists other works by the same author

19. What was Evelyn's biggest challenge as a child?

_____

_____

_____

_____

_____

_____

_____

_____

_____

20. Evelyn Cisneros has received many awards from Hispanic organizations because

_____

_____

_____

_____

_____

_____

_____

_____

_____

_____

_____

© Harcourt

Off and Running

Directions: For items 1–18, fill in the circle in front of the correct answer. For items 19–20, write the answer.

Vocabulary

1. Because he is excited about the election, my father put a _____ sticker on his car.
   - Ⓐ residences
   - Ⓑ campaign
   - Ⓒ graffiti
   - Ⓓ science

2. The traffic noise was so _____ that we closed our doors to avoid hearing it.
   - Ⓐ endorse
   - Ⓑ campaign
   - Ⓒ obnoxious
   - Ⓓ enlightened

3. Volunteers are covering the _____ on the walls with a fresh coat of paint.
   - Ⓐ graffiti
   - Ⓑ residence
   - Ⓒ campaign
   - Ⓓ fear

4. After we move next week, our new _____ will be at 12 Vernon Lane.
   - Ⓐ obnoxious
   - Ⓑ endorse
   - Ⓒ graffiti
   - Ⓓ residence

5. Dad will _____ Sal Regis for the new mayor of our town.
   - Ⓐ campaign
   - Ⓑ endorse
   - Ⓒ residence
   - Ⓓ danger

Comprehension

6. You know this selection is realistic fiction because _____ .
   - Ⓐ the characters and events are like people and events in real life
   - Ⓑ many of the events are not realistic
   - Ⓒ it takes place in an unreal world
   - Ⓓ it tells about Hispanic culture

7. Why is Miata telephoning her classmates?

  Ⓐ to ask for help with her aquarium

  Ⓑ to get them to make posters and buttons

  Ⓒ to ask them to vote for her in the election

  Ⓓ to ask them to call up other classmates

8. Why does Papi think Miata is calling her boyfriend?

  Ⓐ He hears her talking to someone.

  Ⓑ He knows her boyfriend.

  Ⓒ She tells Papi that she called a boy.

  Ⓓ She has been on the phone a lot.

9. Miata wants to know someone important so that _____ .

  Ⓐ that person can support her for the election

  Ⓑ she can get an autograph

  Ⓒ that person will come to her home

  Ⓓ she can meet a rock star

10. "Her mind began to turn." In this selection, *turn* means to _____ .

  Ⓐ move in circles

  Ⓑ think hard

  Ⓒ bump one's head

  Ⓓ feel ill

11. In this selection, who is the person who says "better than a friend of Rudy's"?

  Ⓐ Papi

  Ⓑ Rudy's best friend

  Ⓒ Rudy himself

  Ⓓ Eddie Olmos

12. Why does Miata want to visit Doña Vasquez?

  Ⓐ Miata is interested in being a mayor.

  Ⓑ Miata likes the woman and wants to see her again.

  Ⓒ Miata knows that she will have a good time.

  Ⓓ Miata wants to know how to win an election.

© Harcourt

Practice Book
Distant Voyages

13. What is Doña Vasquez doing when Miata gets to her house?

Ⓐ fixing a lamp

Ⓑ gardening

Ⓒ making bread

Ⓓ reading the newspaper

14. Why did Doña Vasquez run against her husband for mayor?

Ⓐ She didn't like him.

Ⓑ She thought that she was smarter than he was.

Ⓒ She disagreed with his ideas.

Ⓓ She was young.

15. Doña Carmen's husband was against hiring the teacher from Mexico City because _____ .

Ⓐ she was a woman

Ⓑ she spoke only Spanish

Ⓒ her city ideas were good for the children

Ⓓ her ideas would make the children bad

16. Rudy Herrera thinks that he will win the election because _____ .

Ⓐ he has promised lots of ice cream and more recess time

Ⓑ Miata doesn't have any experience in student government

Ⓒ he is a boy

Ⓓ he thinks he is smarter than Miata

17. Miata wants to improve her school by _____ .

Ⓐ fixing broken equipment

Ⓑ repairing the walls and windows

Ⓒ erasing the graffiti

Ⓓ making the school more beautiful

18. When does Miata see Doña Vasquez's flowers?

Ⓐ before Doña Vasquez talks about being mayor

Ⓑ after Doña Vasquez offers to give her flowers

Ⓒ after Miata tells about her school

Ⓓ before Miata gives her the loaf of bread

19. The story says that Doña Vasquez looked into Miata's heart. Explain what this means.

_____

_____

_____

_____

_____

_____

_____

_____

20. Why does Miata bite her lip when Doña Vasquez asks what her election promise is?

_____

_____

_____

_____

_____

_____

_____

_____

_____

Little by Little

Directions: For items 1–18, fill in the circle in front of the correct answer.
For items 19–20, write the answer.

Vocabulary

1. Because I can't _____ her poor handwriting, I do not know what her letter says.
   - (A) dismay
   - (B) astonish
   - (C) decipher
   - (D) permit

2. Jean did not expect to win, so she was _____ when the judges gave her first prize.
   - (A) deciphered
   - (B) dismay
   - (C) despise
   - (D) astonished

3. The artist looked at his ruined painting with _____ .
   - (A) dismay
   - (B) astonished
   - (C) decipher
   - (D) confession

4. The actor was so convincing as the "bad guy" that everyone _____ him.
   - (A) immobility
   - (B) despised
   - (C) decipher
   - (D) retired

5. The teacher walked with a slight limp because she had had _____ as a child.
   - (A) dismay
   - (B) astonished
   - (C) polio
   - (D) publicity

6. That scare shocked me into _____ .
   - (A) decipher
   - (B) immobility
   - (C) astonished
   - (D) gravelly

Comprehension

7. Why does Jean think that Miss Marr will understand her seeing problem?
   (A) Her teacher is young and pretty.
   (B) Her teacher has a limp.
   (C) Her teacher has a gentle voice.
   (D) Her teacher likes Mr. Johnston.

8. Why does the teacher put Jean's desk right against the front blackboard?
   (A) because there is no other place for it
   (B) because Jean is a discipline problem
   (C) because Jean wants to sit apart from the other students
   (D) because Jean is supposed to see the board better up close

9. Why doesn't Jean explain her reading problem to her teacher?
   (A) because she is embarrassed
   (B) because she doesn't think it is a big problem
   (C) because Miss Marr wouldn't listen to her
   (D) because she doesn't like Miss Marr

10. "Shirley had about her the magic of a story" means Shirley _____ .
    (A) liked stories
    (B) had a lot of books
    (C) seemed to have an interesting life
    (D) knew how to do magic

11. In the selection, Shirley is referred to as the "War Guest herself" because she _____ .
    (A) likes to pick fights on the playground
    (B) lives with her aunt and uncle
    (C) was sent from England to escape the bombings
    (D) has a charming English accent

Practice Book
Distant Voyages

12. Why is Jean excited that Shirley is going to help her?

Ⓐ Jean likes her brother, Ian.

Ⓑ Jean has always wanted to be friends with a girl.

Ⓒ Jean is always looking for someone to help her.

Ⓓ Shirley is from England.

13. Shirley turns out to be _____ .

Ⓐ a very excitable person

Ⓑ a quiet, polite girl

Ⓒ a very good friend to Jean

Ⓓ an unkind person

14. Jean begins talking to a tree after _____ .

Ⓐ Shirley leaves her in the schoolyard

Ⓑ she takes the arithmetic test

Ⓒ she tells Miss Marr what she did

Ⓓ Jamie meets her at school

15. Why doesn't Jean write down a single answer on her test?

Ⓐ She can't write fast enough.

Ⓑ She doesn't know the addition facts.

Ⓒ She doesn't know the multiplication facts.

Ⓓ She doesn't have a pencil.

16. When Jean says that she has all the math problems correct, she feels _____ .

Ⓐ pleased

Ⓑ guilty

Ⓒ excited

Ⓓ disappointed

17. This selection is like an autobiography because it _____ .

Ⓐ tells a true story about an incident in the author's life

Ⓑ tells a story about a time in school

Ⓒ explains why the author is nearly blind

Ⓓ tells about made-up events in a person's life

18. "Ruth and Stella lurked near enough to hear what I said." In this story, *lurked* means that Ruth and Stella _____ .

   Ⓐ sneaked

   Ⓑ kept on staying

   Ⓒ were dangerous

   Ⓓ were hidden

19. What lesson does Jean learn from Miss Marr when she confesses to cheating?

_____

_____

_____

_____

_____

_____

_____

_____

20. How are desks in schools today different from those in Jean's school?

_____

_____

_____

_____

_____

_____

_____

_____

_____

_____

Dear Mr. Henshaw

Directions: For items 1–18, fill in the circle in front of the correct answer.
For items 19–20, write the answer.

Vocabulary

1. Wires are _____ to prevent short circuits from occurring.
   (A) muffle
   (B) submitted
   (C) insulated
   (D) grade

2. We put up a _____ to divide the room into two parts.
   (A) refinery
   (B) grade
   (C) muffle
   (D) partition

3. The tiger _____ in the tall grass, searching for its prey.
   (A) muffles
   (B) submitted
   (C) prowls
   (D) enhances

4. Strong fumes were rising from the nearby oil _____ .
   (A) refinery
   (B) insulated
   (C) partition
   (D) grade

5. The road had a steep _____ , so the truck driver shifted to a lower gear.
   (A) muffle
   (B) grade
   (C) submitted
   (D) partition

6. Because every student in class _____ his or her book report on time, our teacher read us a story.
   (A) prowls
   (B) muffle
   (C) grade
   (D) submitted

7. If you put the alarm clock under a pillow, you will _____ its loud ring.
   (A) insulated
   (B) muffle
   (C) refinery
   (D) devote

Comprehension

8. How can you can tell that Leigh enjoys writing in his diary?

Ⓐ He thinks that will please Mr. Henshaw.

Ⓑ He got a new notebook.

Ⓒ He always has it up-to-date.

Ⓓ He filled up his first notebook.

9. What shows that Leigh is having trouble with an idea for a story?

Ⓐ He is thinking about writing a poem on butterflies.

Ⓑ He needs one more idea for his story about the ten-foot wax man.

Ⓒ He hopes to write about batteries.

Ⓓ He writes a letter to his dad instead of writing a story.

10. Leigh thinks that he can make an alarm because _____ .

Ⓐ he is always inventing things

Ⓑ the hardware man goes to Leigh's house

Ⓒ he has been reading library books on the subject

Ⓓ his dad is an electrician

11. How does the man in the hardware store figure out what Leigh is making?

Ⓐ He sees Leigh walk into the store.

Ⓑ The bell rings in the store.

Ⓒ He hears Leigh talking about what he intends to make.

Ⓓ He notices Leigh's lunchbox and the items he picks out.

12. What does Leigh do when he has a problem with his alarm lunchbox?

Ⓐ buys another lunchbox

Ⓑ asks Barry for help

Ⓒ thinks and experiments

Ⓓ gives up on the whole idea

13. Why can't Leigh wait for Monday to arrive?
  (A) He loves school.
  (B) He is going to find out who stole his lunch.
  (C) He has a new lunchbox with a padlock on it.
  (D) His mom will make salami and cream cheese sandwiches.

14. When does Leigh begin to feel like a hero?
  (A) when everyone wants his lunch
  (B) when he finds out who stole his lunch
  (C) when everyone is interested in the alarm
  (D) when his alarm startles everyone

15. "I dashed off a description of the time I rode with my father." In this selection, *dashed off* means _____ .
  (A) ran after
  (B) wrote and wrote
  (C) put in short lines
  (D) wrote down quickly

16. Why is Leigh mad and disgusted?
  (A) because there are only franks and beans for supper
  (B) because his father sounds lonely
  (C) because his parents aren't married anymore
  (D) because he doesn't know what to say to his father

17. In the Young Writer's contest, Leigh wins _____ .
  (A) first prize
  (B) second prize
  (C) third prize
  (D) honorable mention

18. Mrs. Badger says all the following things are true about Leigh's story **except** _____ .

  Ⓐ he wrote honestly about something he knew about

  Ⓑ Leigh imitated Mr. Henshaw's writing style

  Ⓒ the story was a splendid work for a young writer

  Ⓓ the reader experiences going down a steep hill

19. Why does Leigh want to meet Mrs. Badger?

_____

_____

_____

_____

_____

_____

_____

_____

20. Why is Leigh quiet on the way home?

_____

_____

_____

_____

_____

_____

_____

_____

Directions: For items 1–18, fill in the circle in front of the correct answer.
For items 19–20, write the answer.

Vocabulary

1. The man was so _____ in his thoughts that he did not notice when the traffic light changed from red to green.
   - Ⓐ sidetrack
   - Ⓑ absorbed
   - Ⓒ beaming
   - Ⓓ emptied

2. We walked up and down each _____ at the grocery store, trying to remember all the things we needed for supper.
   - Ⓐ oath
   - Ⓑ reputation
   - Ⓒ aisle
   - Ⓓ vacation

3. To join the club, we had to take an _____, saying that we would not break any club rules.
   - Ⓐ absorbed
   - Ⓑ aisle
   - Ⓒ interested
   - Ⓓ oath

4. Ted's mother could not help _____ with pride as her son performed in the talent show.
   - Ⓐ beaming
   - Ⓑ sidetrack
   - Ⓒ reputation
   - Ⓓ broadly

5. Grace has the _____ of being honest and trustworthy.
   - Ⓐ sidetrack
   - Ⓑ absorbed
   - Ⓒ reputation
   - Ⓓ partition

6. By asking questions, Tim tried to _____ our teacher from giving us a test.
   - Ⓐ absorbed
   - Ⓑ oath
   - Ⓒ reputation
   - Ⓓ sidetrack

Comprehension

7. Nick feels that the worst thing that can happen in class is _____ .

Ⓐ writing a report

Ⓒ giving an oral report

Ⓑ being treated like the teacher's pet

Ⓓ answering the teacher's questions

8. What is the German word for dog?

Ⓐ *chien*

Ⓑ *dog*

Ⓒ *hund*

Ⓓ *perro*

9. What book is Mrs. Granger describing?

Ⓐ a math book

Ⓑ a phone book

Ⓒ a notebook

Ⓓ a dictionary

10. Mrs. Granger gets through the whole day's assignment _____ .

Ⓐ in eight minutes

Ⓑ in French

Ⓒ with great difficulty

Ⓓ without any wrong answers

11. Why is Nick asking Mrs. Granger questions?

Ⓐ to learn words in foreign languages

Ⓑ to learn more about dictionaries

Ⓒ to keep her from giving more homework

Ⓓ to become the teacher's pet

12. What helps Nick understand what Mrs. Granger said about the meaning of words?

Ⓐ an experience he had in preschool

Ⓑ a discussion at the newspaper meeting

Ⓒ his latest assignment from Mrs. Granger

Ⓓ his and Janet's talk about Mrs. Granger's class

Practice Book
Distant Voyages

13. When does Nick understand what Mrs. Granger said about the meaning of words?
    A as he leads the newspaper meeting
    B while he and Janet are walking home
    C after he eats dinner
    D before he leaves school

14. What happens after Nick accidentally knocks Janet off the curb?
    A She picks up the gold pen.
    B She falls on the pavement.
    C He talks about Mrs. Granger's class.
    D He uses the word *frindle* for the first time.

15. Why does Nick ask the lady in the store for a frindle?
    A because he wants to try using *frindle* as a real word
    B because he needs a black pen
    C because Mrs. Granger told the class to buy a special kind of pen
    D because he knows the saleslady speaks German

16. According to the selection, what is Nick's middle name?
    A Frindle
    B Allen
    C Gwagala
    D Action

17. How does Nick try to make *frindle* a real English word?
    A He teaches the word to the clerk at the store.
    B He has his friends take an oath never to say *pen*.
    C He tells Mrs. Granger about a frindle.
    D He finds the word in the book *Words Alive*.

18. Which best describes Nick?
    A dishonest
    B disorganized
    C imaginative
    D musical

Practice Book
Distant Voyages

19. What is Nick's big plan?

_____

_____

_____

_____

_____

_____

_____

_____

_____

20. How does Nick know that his plan is working?

_____

_____

_____

_____

_____

_____

_____

_____

_____

_____

_____

© Harcourt

Practice Book
Distant Voyages

The Fun They Had

Directions: For items 1–18, fill in the circle in front of the correct answer.
For items 19–20, write the answer.

Vocabulary

1. To keep the sun from shining on the chalkboard, the teacher _____ the window blinds.
   - Ⓐ sorrowfully
   - Ⓑ loftily
   - Ⓒ adjusted
   - Ⓓ dispute

2. Our neighbors are having a _____ about the boundary between their property.
   - Ⓐ dispute
   - Ⓑ nonchalantly
   - Ⓒ loftily
   - Ⓓ disagree

3. Maria seemed to walk _____ on stage to give her speech, but her stomach was in knots.
   - Ⓐ dispute
   - Ⓑ nonchalantly
   - Ⓒ adjusted
   - Ⓓ reputation

4. During his campaign, the governor spoke _____ of the changes he was planning to make when he took office.
   - Ⓐ adjusted
   - Ⓑ dispute
   - Ⓒ mournfully
   - Ⓓ loftily

5. _____ we said good-bye to our friends but promised to write when we were settled in our new town.
   - Ⓐ Gravelly
   - Ⓑ Adjusted
   - Ⓒ Dispute
   - Ⓓ Sorrowfully

Comprehension

6. This selection is most like _____ .
   - Ⓐ realistic fiction
   - Ⓑ science fiction
   - Ⓒ a personal narrative
   - Ⓓ a science book

7. When does this selection take place?

　Ⓐ in the past

　Ⓑ in the present day

　Ⓒ within the next couple of months

　Ⓓ in the distant future

8. Tommy and Margie are _____ .

　Ⓐ brother and sister

　Ⓑ neighborhood friends

　Ⓒ cousins

　Ⓓ friends who live far apart

9. Where does Tommy find the "real book"?

　Ⓐ in an old trunk

　Ⓑ in Margie's attic

　Ⓒ in his attic

　Ⓓ in a very old box

10. For Margie, what is the worst part of school?

　Ⓐ taking tests

　Ⓑ handing in her homework and tests

　Ⓒ studying

　Ⓓ her classroom

11. What does Margie dislike about her teacher?

　Ⓐ the big screen

　Ⓑ the test slot

　Ⓒ using punch cards to answer tests

　Ⓓ the speed with which the teacher corrects tests

12. Why has Margie been doing poorly in geography?

　Ⓐ Her teacher has introduced too much material too quickly.

　Ⓑ She has been taking too many tests.

　Ⓒ Her teacher has been away for nearly a month.

　Ⓓ Her teacher taught incorrect information.

© Harcourt

13. Why does Margie say, "I wouldn't want a strange man in my house to teach me"?

Ⓐ She is afraid that the County Inspector will be her substitute teacher.

Ⓑ Tommy's father is going to help her with geography.

Ⓒ She thinks that teachers used to go to students' homes to teach them.

Ⓓ Margie is more comfortable with a woman teacher.

14. How does Tommy act toward Margie?

Ⓐ as though she's more intelligent than he is

Ⓑ as though she is stupid

Ⓒ as if she is as smart as he is

Ⓓ as if she needs to learn her geography

15. How does Tommy compare his teacher to his father?

Ⓐ His father is not as smart as a mechanical teacher.

Ⓑ His father knows as much as his mechanical teacher.

Ⓒ Old-fashioned teachers went to students' houses.

Ⓓ His father can't individualize his teaching.

16. Which of the following is Margie's mother most likely to say?

Ⓐ Children learn best if they choose when they go to school.

Ⓑ All eleven-year-olds should be taught the same things in the same way.

Ⓒ Teachers don't adjust to children. Children adjust to teachers.

Ⓓ Because each child learns differently, each child should be taught differently.

17. For which of the following reasons does Margie think that the old schools were fun?

Ⓐ The students never had to take tests.

Ⓑ The teachers were people.

Ⓒ Students had lots of opportunities to be together.

Ⓓ The grading system was easier.

Practice Book
Distant Voyages

18. Which saying best suits this story?

(A) The grass is always greener on the other side of the fence.

(B) Don't shut the barn door after the horse has run away.

(C) Don't cry over spilled milk.

(D) Where there's a will, there's a way.

19. How is the teacher in the real book different from Margie's teacher?

_____

_____

_____

_____

_____

_____

_____

_____

20. List two reasons why the real book seems strange to Tommy and Margie.

_____

_____

_____

_____

_____

_____

_____

_____

_____

Practice Book
Distant Voyages

Across the Wide Dark Sea

Directions: For items 1–18, fill in the circle in front of the correct answer.
For items 19–20, write the answer.

Vocabulary

1. Caught in the snowstorm, we _____ together to stay warm.
   Ⓐ lurked   Ⓑ vast
   Ⓒ huddled   Ⓓ furl

2. The pioneers looked out over the _____ prairie and knew it would take
them days to cross it.
   Ⓐ beams   Ⓑ huddled
   Ⓒ lurked   Ⓓ vast

3. The lone wolf _____ in the shadows near the sheep pen.
   Ⓐ rigging   Ⓑ lurked
   Ⓒ furl   Ⓓ adjusted

4. The sailors climbed the _____ as the tall ship pulled into port.
   Ⓐ rigging   Ⓑ vast
   Ⓒ settlement   Ⓓ background

5. In olden days, everyone helped raise the _____ for a new barn at
barn-raising parties.
   Ⓐ rigging   Ⓑ furl
   Ⓒ beams   Ⓓ huddled

6. The sailors had to _____ the sails to keep them from ripping in the storm.
   Ⓐ lurked   Ⓑ furl
   Ⓒ vast   Ⓓ beams

7. The pioneers cleared the land so they could start a _____ near the river.
   Ⓐ settlement   Ⓑ rigging
   Ⓒ beams   Ⓓ reputation

Comprehension

8. This selection is most like historical fiction because _____ .
- (A) people's names weren't mentioned in the story
- (B) storms come up at sea all the time
- (C) people could not live that long on the *Mayflower*
- (D) the *Mayflower* really sailed to America

9. Why do the faces of the people on shore grow smaller and smaller?
- (A) The people are all very short.
- (B) The ship is sailing away from them.
- (C) The people on the ship don't have good eyesight.
- (D) The people on shore are running away.

10. The living quarters on the ship are _____ .
- (A) bright and cheery
- (B) large enough
- (C) full of space
- (D) very crowded

11. Why is the storyteller's family luckier than most?
- (A) They have a dry corner.
- (B) They are damp and cold.
- (C) They sleep in a work boat.
- (D) They are packed in tightly.

12. What does the family eat at sea?
- (A) beans, hamburgers, and bread
- (B) salt pork, beans, and bread
- (C) peanut butter, jelly, and beans
- (D) roast pork and string beans

© Harcourt

Practice Book
Distant Voyages

13. Which phrase helps you best picture the fierce storm?

   Ⓐ a stiff wind

   Ⓑ catching hold of a rope

   Ⓒ raging, foaming water

   Ⓓ not too stormy

14. The ship begins to leak due to _____ .

   Ⓐ the many storms it has gone through

   Ⓑ its weight

   Ⓒ an iron jack falling on it

   Ⓓ the number of people on board

15. *Rigging, mast,* and *main beam* can be grouped as _____ .

   Ⓐ parts of a ship

   Ⓑ passengers' supplies

   Ⓒ kinds of birds

   Ⓓ sailors' equipment

16. Why do people begin to question their reasons for going on this journey?

   Ⓐ Their clothes are always wet.

   Ⓑ The voyage is so difficult.

   Ⓒ They are running out of food.

   Ⓓ The sailors are very rude.

17. All the following are evidence of land being nearby **except** _____ .

   Ⓐ seaweed   Ⓑ tree branches

   Ⓒ clouds   Ⓓ feathers

18. When does the storyteller's mother cry and smile at the same time?

   Ⓐ when she eats fresh food

   Ⓑ when she sees land ahead

   Ⓒ when her son gets better

   Ⓓ when the ship leaves port

19. Why does a small party of men go ashore first?

_____

_____

_____

_____

_____

_____

_____

_____

20. Why did the author write this story?

_____

_____

_____

_____

_____

_____

_____

_____

_____

Name This American

Directions: For items 1–18, fill in the circle in front of the correct answer. For items 19–20, write the answer.

Vocabulary

1. Before the ball game began, we all stood to sing the national _____ .
   - Ⓐ interpreter
   - Ⓑ guarantee
   - Ⓒ suffrage
   - Ⓓ anthem

2. Our principal was proud to introduce the _____ guest speaker to our school.
   - Ⓐ misleading
   - Ⓑ distinguished
   - Ⓒ interpreter
   - Ⓓ suffrage

3. If you are good at learning languages, you might want to become an _____ .
   - Ⓐ indebted
   - Ⓑ anthem
   - Ⓒ interpreter
   - Ⓓ instant

4. Our family is _____ to everyone in the community for all that was done to help us in our time of need.
   - Ⓐ indebted
   - Ⓑ stumps
   - Ⓒ suffrage
   - Ⓓ misleading

5. In the early 1900s, many women worked diligently to ensure that _____ for women would become a reality.
   - Ⓐ guarantee
   - Ⓑ suffrage
   - Ⓒ stumps
   - Ⓓ settlement

6. That question is so difficult, it _____ even the experts.
   - Ⓐ indebted
   - Ⓑ misleading
   - Ⓒ stumps
   - Ⓓ guarantee

7. Can you _____ that we will have the same seats for the playoff games?
   - Ⓐ guarantee
   - Ⓑ distinguished
   - Ⓒ interpreter
   - Ⓓ indebted

8. His answer to my question was vague and _____ .

Ⓐ indebted   Ⓑ distinguished

Ⓒ guarantee   Ⓓ misleading

Comprehension

9. If this play were a television program, it would be a _____ .

Ⓐ cartoon   Ⓑ game show

Ⓒ news report   Ⓓ comedy show

10. Walter Hunt invented the _____ .

Ⓐ bread box   Ⓑ comb

Ⓒ pen   Ⓓ safety pin

11. The sculptor who carved the presidents' faces in Mount Rushmore was _____ .

Ⓐ Uncle Sam   Ⓑ Dolley Madison

Ⓒ Gutzon Borglum   Ⓓ Babe Ruth

12. What does Dolley Madison remember most about entertaining at the White House?

Ⓐ serving ice cream for the first time

Ⓑ being the First Lady

Ⓒ entertaining important people

Ⓓ spending money

13. Sacajawea tries to trick the panel by _____ .

Ⓐ dressing in men's clothing

Ⓑ making jokes

Ⓒ speaking in a deep voice

Ⓓ not speaking at all

14. In the Shoshone language, *Sacajawea* means _____ .

   Ⓐ Bird Woman

   Ⓑ explorer

   Ⓒ Indian guide

   Ⓓ river

15. One of Elizabeth Cady Stanton's biggest accomplishments was _____ .

   Ⓐ being elected to Congress

   Ⓑ carving Mount Rushmore

   Ⓒ finding a new comet

   Ⓓ demanding voting rights for women

16. Babe Ruth set baseball records for _____ .

   Ⓐ most errors in one game

   Ⓑ both pitching and hitting

   Ⓒ pitching only

   Ⓓ hitting only

17. Which panelist was a queen?

   Ⓐ Liliuokalani

   Ⓑ Elizabeth Cady Stanton

   Ⓒ Sacajawea

   Ⓓ Dolley Madison

18. Why might the program's sponsor have chosen Uncle Sam as the host of the show?

   Ⓐ He is a famous football player.

   Ⓑ He said he would do it for free.

   Ⓒ He is a symbol of the United States.

   Ⓓ He is a famous soldier.

19. Why do the panelists need to know something about United States history?

_____

_____

_____

_____

_____

_____

_____

_____

_____

20. The play includes several famous Americans. Name the person who belongs in each of these groups—scientist, queen, president's wife, inventor, baseball player, artist, supporter of women's rights, western guide.

_____

_____

_____

_____

_____

_____

_____

_____

_____

_____

_____

_____

© Harcourt

What's the Big Idea, Ben Franklin?

Directions: For items 1–18, fill in the circle in front of the correct answer.
For items 19–20, write the answer.

Vocabulary

1. Is this the most recent _____ of the book?
- Ⓐ edition
- Ⓑ treaty
- Ⓒ honors
- Ⓓ suspended

2. Balloons and streamers were _____ from the ceiling to make the room look festive.
- Ⓐ honors
- Ⓑ contraption
- Ⓒ suspended
- Ⓓ shortened

3. The astronaut received several _____ at the ceremony.
- Ⓐ treaty
- Ⓑ honors
- Ⓒ suspended
- Ⓓ repeal

4. The senators are trying to _____ the ineffective law.
- Ⓐ suspended
- Ⓑ repeal
- Ⓒ honors
- Ⓓ edition

5. The pioneers signed a _____ with the Indians promising not to settle beyond the river.
- Ⓐ treaty
- Ⓑ repeal
- Ⓒ contraption
- Ⓓ suspended

6. My grandfather rigged up a _____ that would open and shut to let our dog go in and out of the house.
- Ⓐ suspended
- Ⓑ contraption
- Ⓒ repeal
- Ⓓ treaty

Practice Book
Distant Voyages

Comprehension

7. "Every family bought an almanac each year." In this selection, an *almanac* is a _____.

Ⓐ comic book   Ⓑ book of information

Ⓒ book of songs   Ⓓ book of stories

8. Why didn't Franklin's electrical picnic go as planned?

Ⓐ The turkey ran away.

Ⓑ A goose was cooked.

Ⓒ Franklin was knocked unconscious.

Ⓓ Franklin had to perform magic tricks.

9. Why couldn't Franklin do the electricity experiment in Philadelphia?

Ⓐ He wasn't in Europe.

Ⓑ No place in Philadelphia was high enough.

Ⓒ There weren't many storms there.

Ⓓ Dangerous scientific experiments were not allowed there.

10. Why did Franklin become the most famous person in the American colonies?

Ⓐ He started publishing an almanac.

Ⓑ He represented the American colonies in England.

Ⓒ His ideas proved that electricity and lightning are the same thing.

Ⓓ He represented the American colonies in France.

11. Who gave Franklin the title of doctor?

Ⓐ different universities

Ⓑ the kings of England and France

Ⓒ newspapers

Ⓓ three scientists in Europe

12. Franklin invented the lightning rod, a pointed iron rod that could be attached to the roof of a building. In this selection, a lightning rod is _____ .

Ⓐ an instrument that protects buildings from lightning

Ⓑ an iron rod that is used for decoration

Ⓒ a rod that is used to photograph lightning

Ⓓ a kind of doorbell

Practice Book
Distant Voyages

13. Franklin improved life for the people of Philadelphia by helping to establish _____ .

  (A) a company to make lightning rods

  (B) a hospital and a new congress

  (C) better postal service to England

  (D) a fire insurance company and a hospital

14. At different times in his life, Franklin represented the American colonies in both England and France. What ability earned Franklin these jobs?

  (A) his storytelling skills

  (B) his talent in looking like a rich man

  (C) his scientific knowledge

  (D) his skill in persuading people

15. How did Franklin act differently in England than in France?

  (A) In England he dressed stylishly, and in France he did not.

  (B) He wore fancy eyeglasses in France but not in England.

  (C) In England he did not follow the rules of good behavior as he did in France.

  (D) In England he dressed plainly, and in France he wore a fur hat.

16. Franklin's last public duty was to _____ .

  (A) help write the Declaration of Independence

  (B) organize a new mail system between Boston and Philadelphia

  (C) help write the Constitution of the United States

  (D) get France's help for the American Revolution

17. What was Franklin's opinion of the Constitution?

  (A) was very dissatisfied with the way it was written

  (B) thought it was the best possible document, considering the situation

  (C) approved of it completely

  (D) supported a different kind of government

18. All the following are true about Franklin **except** that _____ .

   Ⓐ he worked hard for American independence from England

   Ⓑ he was not interested in practical uses for scientific ideas

   Ⓒ he had many different kinds of abilities

   Ⓓ he enjoyed eating and dressing well

19. What was George Washington's job during the American Revolution? What was Franklin's job at the same time?

_____

_____

_____

_____

_____

_____

_____

20. Why did the author include both serious and funny information about Franklin?

_____

_____

_____

_____

_____

_____

© Harcourt

Lewis and Clark

Directions: For items 1–18, fill in the circle in front of the correct answer. For items 19–20, write the answer.

Vocabulary

1. When my sister received a scholarship, she _____ cried tears of joy.
   - Ⓐ dismal
   - Ⓑ peril
   - Ⓒ profusely
   - Ⓓ loftily

2. Driving up the mountain, we traveled over rough and hilly _____ .
   - Ⓐ terrain
   - Ⓑ peril
   - Ⓒ ordeal
   - Ⓓ tangles

3. With all the road construction in our town, driving has became a terrible _____ .
   - Ⓐ esteem
   - Ⓑ ordeal
   - Ⓒ dismal
   - Ⓓ oath

4. The days grew more and more _____ as the heavy rains continued day after day.
   - Ⓐ profusely
   - Ⓑ dismal
   - Ⓒ terrain
   - Ⓓ pelting

5. The young artist's painting was held in high _____ by the older art critics.
   - Ⓐ dismal
   - Ⓑ profusely
   - Ⓒ ordeal
   - Ⓓ esteem

6. The lack of rain put the woods in _____ of fires.
   - Ⓐ peril
   - Ⓑ terrain
   - Ⓒ ordeal
   - Ⓓ esteem

Comprehension

7. Seeing the top of the Rocky Mountains was both inspiring and troubling to Lewis and Clark because _____ .
- Ⓐ the mountains were so far away
- Ⓑ they knew the mountains would be difficult to cross
- Ⓒ the mountain tops were covered with snow
- Ⓓ they had to carry their boats over the Great Falls first

8. How did Lewis describe the Great Falls?
- Ⓐ the greatest obstacle I have ever faced
- Ⓑ as high as a six-story building
- Ⓒ the greatest sight I ever beheld
- Ⓓ impossible to conquer without Sacagawea

9. Sacagawea proved to be a valuable asset to the expedition because she _____ .
- Ⓐ carefully scanned the riverbanks
- Ⓑ had been a slave-child long ago
- Ⓒ hiked ahead of the party
- Ⓓ helped the captains select the correct rivers to travel

10. Why were the Shoshone women "frozen with fear" when Lewis met them?
- Ⓐ They only trusted their neighbors, the Blackfeet.
- Ⓑ Lewis wanted to buy horses from them.
- Ⓒ They had never seen other people before.
- Ⓓ They were suspicious of all outsiders.

11. Sacagawea cried when she saw Chief Cameahwait because he _____ .
- Ⓐ was her brother
- Ⓑ had scared her
- Ⓒ had kidnapped her long ago
- Ⓓ was her father

Practice Book
Distant Voyages

12. Lewis and Clark thought that all the streams on the far side of the Rockies would _____ .

   Ⓐ flow directly into the Pacific Ocean

   Ⓑ flow into the Columbia

   Ⓒ destroy their beat-up canoes

   Ⓓ be filled with schools of fish

13. The land around the Columbia River was later called the _____ .

   Ⓐ Ouragon Land   Ⓑ Oregon Territory

   Ⓒ Origan River   Ⓓ Missouri Territory

14. When Lewis and Clark met the Chinook Indians, how did the explorers know they were near the Pacific Ocean?

   Ⓐ Chinook Indians spoke English and told them they were near it.

   Ⓑ Lewis and Clark could see the Pacific Ocean in the distance.

   Ⓒ A Chinook wore a navy jacket, so that meant sailors had been there.

   Ⓓ Nez Perce Indians told them the Chinook Indians lived by the sea.

15. What did Lewis and Clark prove by their expedition?

   Ⓐ No inland waterway existed in North America.

   Ⓑ Their journey was almost a failure.

   Ⓒ Jefferson was pleased with Lewis and Clark.

   Ⓓ They opened the West to settlers by drawing maps.

16. How long did Lewis and Clark's expedition take?

   Ⓐ more than five years

   Ⓑ more than two years

   Ⓒ almost ten years

   Ⓓ less than two years

17. Why was President Jefferson's letter of credit never used?

   Ⓐ The ship's captain let them sail for free.

   Ⓑ No ship ever came into port for six months.

   Ⓒ The letter was stolen by the Indians.

   Ⓓ Sacagawea and her husband took them to the Mandan village.

18. The expedition of Lewis and Clark began and ended _____ .
- (A) in St. Louis, Missouri
- (B) on the Columbia River
- (C) in present-day Astoria, Oregon
- (D) in Washington, D.C.

19. Why did the explorers on the Lewis and Clark expedition "laugh out loud" when they arrived in the Clearwater River Valley?

_____

_____

_____

_____

_____

_____

_____

20. Which part of the Lewis and Clark journey was the most difficult? Tell why you think so.

_____

_____

_____

_____

_____

_____

_____

© Harcourt

Directions: For items 1–18, fill in the circle in front of the correct answer.
For items 19–20, write the answer.

Vocabulary

1. The mole _____ into the ground to escape from its enemy.
   - Ⓐ designated
   - Ⓒ bought
   - Ⓑ exodus
   - Ⓓ burrowed

2. When the fire bell rang, there was an immediate _____ of students out of the classroom.
   - Ⓐ installment
   - Ⓒ exodus
   - Ⓑ designated
   - Ⓓ extinction

3. We paid for the new washing machine in _____ of ten dollars each week.
   - Ⓐ regular
   - Ⓒ migrate
   - Ⓑ installments
   - Ⓓ settlements

4. The flock of birds _____ from the cold weather of the North to the warmer climate of the South.
   - Ⓐ migrated
   - Ⓒ burrowed
   - Ⓑ designated
   - Ⓓ simmered

5. The townspeople _____ a special spot in the park to honor the war heroes of the town.
   - Ⓐ installments
   - Ⓒ burrowed
   - Ⓑ designated
   - Ⓓ astonished

Comprehension

6. The selection is most like a photo essay because it _____ .
   - Ⓐ tells how to do something
   - Ⓑ combines photos and text to present information
   - Ⓒ tells about an event in the first person
   - Ⓓ tells about places of the past

7. Pioneers in Kansas and Nebraska built homes made of _____ .

   Ⓐ trees   Ⓑ sod

   Ⓒ straw   Ⓓ brick

8. The main problem with the soddies was that they _____ .

   Ⓐ were too small

   Ⓑ had no floors

   Ⓒ were built with sod busters

   Ⓓ often leaked during rainstorms

9. According to the selection, people in North and South Dakota often burrowed into the ground under an earthen roof because _____ .

   Ⓐ it was less expensive to live that way

   Ⓑ it helped to keep out some of the severe cold

   Ⓒ they liked living underground in the dark

   Ⓓ the cows and goats lived on the roof

10. To keep a fire going, pioneer women often burned _____ .

   Ⓐ buffalo chips   Ⓑ buffalo hides

   Ⓒ matches   Ⓓ newspaper

11. In the Southwest, women learned from the Indians how to make soap and shampoo from _____ .

   Ⓐ wild grasses   Ⓑ the yucca plant

   Ⓒ buffalo chips   Ⓓ adobe

12. According to the selection, *adobe* houses were built from _____ .

   Ⓐ soap and water   Ⓑ trees and leaves

   Ⓒ sod and mud   Ⓓ mud and straw

13. Benjamin Singleton bought part of a Cherokee reservation to start an all-black community during the years _____ .

   Ⓐ before the Civil War

   Ⓑ during the Civil War

   Ⓒ after the Civil War

   Ⓓ after Nicodemus was built

Practice Book
Distant Voyages

14. By 1879, 800 homesteaders who had left the Old South had _____ .

   (A) moved to Israel

   (B) fought in the Civil War

   (C) come to Kansas to live

   (D) left Kansas for Nebraska and Oklahoma

15. The white farmers already in Kansas saw how hard the new homesteaders worked, so the white farmers _____ .

   (A) loaned them equipment to make their work easier

   (B) told them they would become good farmers

   (C) told them where they could buy equipment

   (D) had them all over for a party

16. George Washington Bush went to the Oregon Territory and _____ .

   (A) built three new black communities

   (B) introduced the first mower and reaper

   (C) suggested using mules to plow the fields

   (D) showed the blacks how to play baseball

17. Nicodemus and Dunlap celebrated Emancipation Day each year by having _____ .

   (A) square dancing and fireworks

   (B) boxing matches and baseball games

   (C) swimming events and gymnastics

   (D) acting and singing classes

18. In 1907, the town of Nicodemus started _____ .

   (A) to be settled by black homesteaders

   (B) their own special holiday celebrations

   (C) recording the town's history

   (D) their own all-black baseball team

Practice Book
Distant Voyages

19. Why was Nicodemus, Kansas, named a National Historical Landmark?

_____

_____

_____

_____

_____

_____

_____

_____

_____

20. It was very difficult to travel so far to live, but the Exodusters did so because

_____

_____

_____

_____

_____

_____

_____

_____

_____

_____

© Harcourt